Women Managers in Neoliberal Japan

This book is about the varying difficulties experienced by women with professional careers in post-bubble Japan, where they are persistently treated by the state and employers as a pool of cheap, contingent resources for the benefit of the broader economy, that is, convenient tools for meeting the government's economic plans on 'womenomics.' Based on ethnographic data gathered from interviews with 160 women managers over a period of nearly 18 years of fieldwork, this study analyses how precarity is produced, reinforced, and perpetuated by continuities and discontinuities in shifting structural processes that generate and perpetuate the experiences of angst, anxiety, frustrations, disillusionment, and insecurity for this segment of the white-collar workforce.

To be women managers in a society that assiduously assigns women's rightful place to the domestic realm in their roles as wives and mothers is to subject their behaviour, choices, and aspirations to scrutiny and criticisms. Women managers are also peripheral, non-core players in the corporate workplace, where opportunities for career advancement are limited, and work conditions become incrementally more difficult with the rise of managerialism and nominal management in the increasingly flexible work environment of today.

With weak in labour unions to offer them limited access to collective representations, and ineffective legislations that provide little protection from unfair or abusive corporate practices, the risks many women face in their pursuit of management-track careers far outweigh the rewards promised by the opportunities they receive. Women's greater access to managerial work in neoliberal Japan is thus a mixed blessing, with significant ramifications on their emotional health, psychological well-being, social relations, and senses of self-worth.

In scrutinizing the contradictions, ambivalence, and conflicts in the lives of women managers in Japan, where neoliberal values are implemented in particular and arbitrary ways for economic agendas, this research offers unique and rich insights into understanding how womenomics as an ideological tool that persistently values women primarily and solely as contingent labour contributes to conflicts of identity and socio-economic precarity for women pursuing management-track careers in the neoliberal work environment today.

Swee-Lin Ho is Associate Professor of Anthropology in the Department of Sociology at the National University of Singapore. Her research interests include the neoliberal transformations of work, new practices of friendship; changing cityscapes and the urban night space; ethnographic field methods and 'studying up' approach; globalization of East Asian popular culture; emergent corporate cultures; the commercialization of intimacy; social formations of gender; and the political economy of the global classical music industry.

She worked for many years in various international cities as auditor, financial journalist, and corporate executive before completing her graduate studies at Sophia University and later the University of Oxford. She has taught in South Korea, where she was also a Korea Foundation Research Fellow studying the conflicting desires of gendered selfhood, nationhood, and cultural identities through the globalization of contemporary Korean popular culture.

Japan Anthropology Workshop Series

Series editor: *Joy Hendry, Oxford Brookes University*

The Japanese Family
Touch, Intimacy and Feeling
Diana Tahhan

Happiness and the Good Life in Japan
Edited by Wolfram Manzenreiter and Barbara Holthus

Religion in Japanese Daily Life
David C. Lewis

Escaping Japan
Reflections on Estrangement and Exile in the Twenty-First Century
Edited by Blai Guarné and Paul Hansen

Women Managers in Neoliberal Japan
Gender, Precarious Labour and Everyday Lives
Swee-Lin Ho

For a full list of available titles please visit: https://www.routledge.com/Japan-Anthropology-Workshop-Series/book-series/SE0627

Women Managers in Neoliberal Japan

Gender, Precarious Labour and Everyday Lives

Swee-Lin Ho

Routledge
Taylor & Francis Group
LONDON AND NEW YORK

First published 2020 by Routledge

2 Park Square, Milton Park, Abingdon, Oxon OX14 4RN
605 Third Avenue, New York, NY 10017

Routledge is an imprint of the Taylor & Francis Group, an informa business

First issud in paperback 2021

Publisher's Note

The publisher has gone to great lengths to ensure the quality of this reprint but points out that some imperfections in the original copies may be apparent.

British Library Cataloguing-in-Publication Data
A catalogue record for this book is available from the British Library

Library of Congress Cataloging-in-Publication Data
A catalog record has been requested for this book

ISBN: 978-0-367-18621-0 (hbk)
ISBN: 978-1-03-217461-7 (pbk)
DOI: 10.4324/9780429197246

Typeset in Times New Roman
by codeMantra

Contents

Tables

Acknowledgements

With nearly 18 years in the making, this book has received an incredible amount of support and insights from an endless list of people since the research began in January 2002.

I am profoundly grateful to David H. Slater for being a constant source of inspiration, an extraordinary teacher, a firm friend, and my fiercest critic since my graduate student days in the School of Comparative Studies (now Faculty of Liberal Arts) at Sophia University. He has helped me discover Anthropology, altered the ways I understand the lives of individuals, and made me a much better ethnographer and person. I also thank many faculty and staff members at Sophia University and The Institute of Comparative Culture for their kind support and encouragement.

I am immensely grateful to Roger Goodman for his unwavering support, guidance, and inspiration since my doctoral studies at The Institute of Social and Cultural Anthropology (ISCA) of the University of Oxford, and without whom this project and book would not have been possible. I thank David Gellner, Ann Waswo, and many other faculty members too for their invaluable advice and encouragement which made graduate life in Oxford a life-changing experience.

I owe special thanks to Joy Hendry for her valuable insights and support over the years. I also thank Peter Sowden, Glenda S. Roberts, and advisers of the Japan Anthropology Workshop Series for their close readings of and detailed comments on the manuscript to significantly improve the scope and depth of the book. Their kind patience and support, together with the efficient management of members of the editorial team at Routledge, have made the entire writing process an enjoyable experience.

Peter Langan was a wonderful colleague and an uncompromisingly dedicated editor during those years when I was a correspondent at Bloomberg News, and has since been a remarkably inspiring mentor and kind friend. His intellectual dynamism, tenacity, and sense of humour have been, and will always be, an important guiding light to navigate me well through calm and difficult times in life.

For the friendship, inspiration, companionship, encouragement, and generosity given to me over two decades of moving around as a 'global homeless citizen,' I express my deepest gratitude to Anne Allison, Atsuta Keiko, Terence Boon, Hironori and Hisami Buma, Peter Cave, Joan Chan, Pauline Chan, Veronica Chan, Chew-Yeo Chor Siang, Chua Khai Woon, Colin Chung, Fujimura Yoshie, Tullia Gianoncelli, Maralee Gibson, Goh Geok Yian; Hagiwara Junko, Hirano Mari, Ho Pui Kam, Horiguchi Sachiko, Christine Hui, Frank Hui, Judy Hui, Iida Junko, Imoto Yuki, Vien Ip, Kariya Takehiko, Kihara Keiko, Kim Hyun Mee, Kimura Mayumi, Kitazume Koji, Mona Leong, Bee G. Lim, Betty Lim, Mary Lee, Brenda Lim, Wendy Lim, Lisa Liu, Lola Martinez, John N. Miksic, Mikura Junichiro and Keiko, Miteri Miko, Miyazaki Silvio, Iman Morooka-Elsamny, Nishigori Hiroshi and Makiko, Nonami Yuri, Oishi Marii, Angela Pang, Shibata Taeko, Tse Wai Ling, Ueno Chizuko, Utsuki Miki, Roxana Waterson, David and Mika Willis, Yamazaki Akiko, Yamazaki Haruko, Yoon Mi Kyung, Yoshida Hitomi, and Yuzawa Kiyomi.

This research has received generous financial support from many sources. They include, in Oxford, the Philip Bagby Scholarship (ISCA), Post-Graduate Scholarship (ISCA), Japan Foundation Endowment, Sasakawa Foundation Scholarship, Carr and Stahl Travel Scholarship (St Antony's College), and E.O. James Bequest Fund (All Souls' College). In Japan, they include the Watanuki International Foundation Scholarship, Sophia University Scholarship, and Adachi Scholarship. Also, the NUS-FASS Writing Fellowship granted by the Faculty of Arts and Social Sciences at the National University of Singapore in 2016 allowed me several months of valuable time away from my teaching commitments to plan and draft the early versions of the manuscript.

I also wish to thank my colleagues in the Department of Sociology at the National University of Singapore (NUS) for their support, encouragement, and engaging discussions, especially Saroja Devi d/o Neyson Dorairajoo, Maribeth Erb, Feng Qiu Shi, Ivan Kwek, Vineeta Sinha, Syed Farid Alatas, Thang Leng Leng, and Eric Thompson.

I appreciate the many invitations to present various aspects of this research over the years which has provided valuable feedback for the book. These include the Institute of Comparative Culture at Sophia University in Tokyo; the International Academic Identities Conference (IAIC) at Hiroshima University; the Institute of Gender Studies at Ochanomizu University in Tokyo; the 15th European Association of Japanese Studies (EAJS) International Conference in Lisbon; the 109th Annual Meeting of the American Anthropological Association (AAA) in Montreal; the Institute of Comparative Culture at Seoul National University; the Inter-Asia Cultural Typhoon Conference at the Tokyo University of Foreign Studies; the Department of Japanese Studies at the University of Hong Kong; the Department of Japanese Studies at the National University of Singapore; the Gender and Media Lecture Series at the University of Oxford; the Asia-Pacific Week at the Australian National University; and the Gender Colloquium at the University of Tokyo.

My most heartfelt gratitude goes to my informants and their family members, friends, and colleagues in Japan for their trust, kindness, and friendship. In opening up their lives, sharing their experiences, and welcoming me warmly to their homes, they have enriched my research, offered me new perspectives on life, and also given me a new home that is at times far better than where I came from.

I dedicate this book to the memory of Marisa Chen, Appy Tang, Suzuki Kazuko, and Yoshida Koichi whose admirable lives had touched those of many, and given inspiration to this book.

This study would not have been conceived or developed into its current form without the constant encouragement, constructive criticisms, affection, and companionship of the extraordinary HZ, who has made this journey of learning and self-discovery most enjoyable, meaningful, and fulfilling.

Note to readers

All informants' names in this book are pseudonyms to protect their identities. The names are presented in the style used in Japan, which begins with the family name and is followed by first name.

Japanese words have been romanized according to the Kenkyūsha's New Japanese-English Dictionary (fifth edition), while abbreviations are used for names of government ministries in the text and in citations, such as MHLW for Ministry of Health, Labour and Welfare, and MOFA for the Ministry of Foreign Affairs.

All Japanese words are italicized or written with appropriate diacritical markings when they occur, such as *pawahara* (power harassment), *okāsan* (mother), and *kūkyo shōshin* (empty promotion). The only exceptions are place names – such as Tokyo, Osaka, and Kyoto – which are not italicized or written with diacritical markings.

The currency in Japan is referred to simply as yen. The sign $ refers to the U.S. dollar, and £ denotes the British pound. For easy reference, all currencies in the book are converted at $1.00 to 108.61 Japanese yen, and at £1.00 to 131.74 yen. The exchange rates are based on the closing foreign exchange spot rates at the end of 30 July 2019 as reported by The Financial Times.

Abbreviations

CC	Civil Code 1896
CCP	Code of Civil Procedure 1998
CEO	Chief Executive Officer
CFA	Chartered Financial Analyst
CFO	Chief Finance Officer
CPA	Certified Public Accountant
EEOL	Equal Employment Opportunity Law 1986
JapanGov	The Government of Japan
JICHIRO	All-Japan Prefectural and Municipal Workers Union
JILPT	Japan Institute of Labour Policy and Training
JLR	Japan Labour Review
LCA	Labor Contract Act 2007
LDAD	Legal Doctrine of Abusive Dismissals
LSA	Labor Standards Act 1947 (Revised 2003)
LTA	Labor Tribunal Act 2004
LUA	Labour Union Act 1947 (Amended 2005)
MIAC	Ministry of Internal Affairs and Communications
MOFA	Ministry of Foreign Affairs
MHLW	Ministry of Health, Labour and Welfare
OECD	Organisation for Economic Co-operation and Development
OPMJ	Office of the Prime Minister, Japan
RENGO	Japanese Trade Union Confederation
SHJ	Statistical Handbook of Japan

Glossary

akuma devil
akuryō evil spirit
anime animations
arubaito part-time job, from the German verb *arbeiten*, which means 'to work'
aruhara alcohol harassment
asobi play
asobi no jidai an era of play
atama ga ii intelligent
baba middle aged or older woman
bābī Barbie doll
baburu bubble (to refer to the economic bubble era in Japan)
baburu no jidai the bubble era
baburu no kodomotachi children of the bubble
baito part-time work (abbreviated form of *arubaito*)
batsu cross, or being given a cross
batsu ichi one cross, or crossed once
batsu ni two crosses, or crossed twice
bijinesu boi business boy
bijinesu gāru business girl
bōnenkai year-end party
bosei maternal
bosei shakai maternal society
bosu boss
buchō head of department or division, at times a director
bugaisha outsiders
Chef: Mitsuboshi no Kyūshoku *Chef: Three Star School Lunch* (TV drama)
chūryū shakai middle-class society
Danjo Koyō Byōdōhō The Equal Employment Opportunity Law 1986
dansei male
dokonimo tsugaranai nagai michi long trail that leads nowhere
dokuritsu independence
Dokuta-X *Doctor-X* (TV drama)

doragon redī dragon lady
eien no shokuba no hana permanent flower in the workplace
eigyō sales
eigyōman salesman, to mean a man working in sales
eikyū shūshoku lifetime employment
era sugiru too high, senior, distinguished, honourable, or important
erai high, senior, distinguished, honourable, or important
fūfu husband and wife
fūfu kankei marital relation
fujin wives or married women
fujinkai Wives' Club (a society or club for married women)
fukubuchō the deputy head
furekkusu taimu flex time (flexible work hours)
furekkusu wāku flexible work
furendoshippu friendship
furendoshippu netowāku friendship network
furītā 'freeter,' someone who has part-time contingent jobs
fusei shakai paternal society
Fushin no Toki *Times of Distrust* (TV drama)
futsū no onna an ordinary woman
futsū no shigoto an ordinary job
ganbaranakute iiyo to not work hard
ganko stubborn
gensō tekina mokuhyō an elusive goal
genzo illusion
gimu obligations
ginkō ūman female banker
ginkōman banker
giri duties
gōman arrogant
gyakuhara reverse harassment
haha oya mothers
haken part-time or temporary work
hakenshain part-time or temporary workers
han shakai teki anti-social
hanabi viewing of fireworks (in the summer)
hanami cherry-blossom viewing
hataraku dansei working men
hataraku josei working woman (a woman who works)
hataraku ningen working person
hazukashii embarrassing or to be embarrassed
herupā-san helper (such as a domestic helper or babysitter)
hikkikomori a self-imposed alienated person
hontō real, genuine

hontō na otona real adults
hontō na tomodachi real friend or friends
hontō na watashi the real me
ibasho a place that offers a sense of belonging
ichininmae a complete person (who is mature and responsible)
ie household, or home
iemoto head of a household
ii otōsan good father
ijime bullying
ikidomari dead-end
inaka mono country bumpkin
inaka musume country girl
ippan shoku ordinary work, as in having a full-time job in an office
izakaya Japanese-style restaurant
jendāhara gender harassment
jibun self
jibunrashī of one's own choice or style
jibunrashī seikatsu lifestyle of one's own choice
jidai period, time, or era
jiji old man
jikan time
jikohakken self-discovery
jimu shoku clerical work
jiritsu independence
josei female
Josei Union Tokyo Women's Union Tokyo
jūjitsukan self-fulfillment
kachi gumi group for winners
kachi inu winner dogs
kachō section chief
kagayaku to shine
kagayaku josei shiny women
kagyō family businesses
Kaikoken Ranyō Hōri Legal Doctrine of Abusive Dismissals
kaisha company
kakarichō supervisor
kanjō emotions
kanjō teki na kyori emotional distance
kanpeki perfect
kanri management
kanrisha manager
kanrishoku a managerial position
kantokusha supervisor
karoshi death from overwork

karyū shakai downward-drifting or sinking society
Katagoshi no Koibito *Over-the-Shoulder Lover* (TV drama)
kazoku family
kazoku kokka the state as family
kazu quantity
keigo honorific language
kekkon marriage
kigyō business, or company
kigyō kumiai company unionism
kikokushijo returnees
Kinkyu Torishirabe Shitsu *Emergency Interrogation Room* (TV drama)
kitai expectations
kodoku solitary
kodomo child, or children
kodomo no umu kikai childbearing machines, or birth-giving machines
kodomotachi children
kojinka process of individuation
kokoro no tomo friends of the heart (beloved friends)
komakai trivial
konkatsu shippaishita josei women who have failed in marriage
kōshi no bunri separation between the public and the private
koshikake chair, temporary seat or transitory job
Koshonin *The Negotiator* (TV drama)
kowai scary or frightening
kūkan space
kūkyo shōshin empty promotion
kūkyo shōshin an empty promotion
kurabu club
kurisumasu kēki Christmas cake (someone who has exceeded the marriageable age of 25)
kusobaba nasty women
kusojiji nasty old men
kyaria career
kyaria daun career down, ' which means taking up job positions of lower status and salary
kyaria kīpu career keep, ' meaning to keep their career
kyaria ūman career woman
kyaria uppu to advance one's career
kyōiku mama educating mothers
kyori distance
mai homu my home
majo witch
make gumi group for losers
make inu loser dog

mama-san mother (women who manage hostess clubs and entertainment venues)
manējā manager
manējā no mane imitating a manager
manga comics
maru round, or whole
matahara maternity harassment, or harassment relating to women's roles as mother
meiro maze
meiwaku wo kakeru mono someone who is a nuisance to others
mendōkusai tiresome or burdensome
mezurashii rare
miai kekkon arranged marriage
mizushōbai water business, or entertainment venues for drinking and voyeuristic play
modorenai to be unable to return or turn back
mongaikan amateurs
Monsuta Parento *Monster Parent* (TV drama)
Morahara moral harassment
nabakari kanrishoku a 'name only' or nominal managerial position
naishoku private jobs
nenkō jōretsu seniority promotion
netowāku network
niau appropriate, compatible, suitable or what feels right
Nihon Rōdōkumiai Sōrengōkai Japanese Trade Union Confederation (RENGO)
nihonjin Japanese people
nihonjinron theories about the Japanese people and Japanese society
nihonshu Japanese rice wine
nijikai second round (usually of drinking)
nītto NEET, or 'Not in Education, Employment or Training'
nomunikēshon communication over drinks
ofisu no okāsan mother in the office
ōgon jidai golden age or era
ohitori sama solitary customers
ojisan middle-aged and older men
okane money
okāsan mother
OL office ladies (doing secretarial or administrative work)
omiai matchmaking
onēsan older sister
oni demon
onibaba demonic hag
onibaba kai group of demonic old hags

onijiji demonic old men
onikuma bear demon
onīsan older brother
Oniyome Nikki *Diary of a Demonic Daughter-in-Law* (TV drama)
onna woman
onna dakara because one is female
onna no shigoto women's job
onna poi like a woman, or feminine
Onna Rōdō Kumiai Kansai Kansai Labour Union for Women
onsen hot spring
otoko man
otoko janai not men, or unmasculine
otoko mitai like a man
otoko no shakai men's world
otokoyaku male role, in a play or performance
otona an adult, or a mature individual
otōsan father
parasaito baba parasite middle-aged women
parasaito onibaba parasite demonic old hags
parasaito shinguru parasite singles
patahara paternity harassment, or harassment relating to men's roles as father
pāto part-time workers
pawā harasumento power harassment
pawahara power harassment
pinku monsuta pink monster, used to describe a female
RENGO Japanese Trade Union Confederation (*Nihon Rōdōkumiai Sōrengōkai*)
Rigaru V: Gen Bengoshi *Legal V: Ex-Lawyer* (TV drama)
Rikon Bengoshi *Divorce Lawyer* (TV drama)
risuhara harassment relating to corporate restructuring
rōgandō impish old men
ryōsai kenbo good wife, wise mother
sabishī lonely
sābisu zangyō free overtime
sakariba an entertainment district full of places to drink, eat, and play
sake a generic term for alcohol, or Japanese rice wine
sanhara three forms of harassment
sanshu no jingi three types of jewels
sararī ūman salaried woman (white-collar female worker)
sararīboi salaried boy, or young office boy
sararīgāru salaried girl, or young office girl
sararīman salaried man (white-collar male worker)
seikai world, international or global

seikaijin an international or global person
seitaigo Empress Dowager Cixi
sekuhara sexual harassment
sengyō shufu professional housewife (full-time housewife)
senmonka experts or specialists
senmu managing director
sensei teacher, or master
sewahara sentiment harassment
shakai society
shakai kengaku an experience of the world outside the home
shakai ni detteta onna women who went out into society (to work)
shakaijin a person or persons in society (a working adult)
shigoto work
shigoto ga jōzu to be good at one's work
shine die (imperative form of the verb *shinu*)
shinguru baba middle-aged, single women
shinnenkai New Year's party
shinu to die
shōbai trade, or business
shōbai onna women in the 'water business' or entertainment industry
shōchū an alcoholic beverage distilled from rice or root vegetables
shokuba no hana flowers placed at a particular site
shokugyō fujin woman with a vocation or occupation
shufu housewife
shunin supervisor
shushin koyō lifetime employment
shūshoku katsudō job-hunting
sobaya-san Japanese restaurant which serves buckwheat noodles
sugiru to exceed, expire, pass by (a point) or be overdue
sūpā super
taka sugiru too expensive
takai expensive
tenjihin item for display
tenshoku job-changing
tesuto test
tokubetsu special, unique
tokubetsu na tomodachi special friends
tomodachi friend
toshi age, year, old, aged
toshi ginkōka investment banker
toshi sugiru too old, or too aged
tsukaenai useless
tsuma wives
wākingu ūman working woman (a woman who works)

wagamana selfish
warikan paying equal share
yakatabune a slim, long, old-styled, Japanese houseboat
yakuin member of a company's board of directors
Yawata no Yabushirazu Yawata's Mystery (a forbidden forest in Chiba prefecture)
yōkai monster
yowai weak
yowai otoko weak man
zangyō overtime
zecchō peak position

1 'Womenomics'

To make women shine or die?

Are women to die for the economy to shine?

It rained unusually hard that Sunday morning in February 2018. All four of us arrived half drenched at the café in Tokyo's Shinjuku[1] district. 'What a heavy downpour!' Hayami Harue[2] exclaims. 'It has been so warm that I had prayed hard for rain, but I did not expect my prayers to be answered like this!' She was quickly teased by her then 24-year-old daughter Hikari[3] who said, 'The rain is good for mother, as she needs to cool down. She has been worried sick about my new job.' Nakao Nyoko laughs at her old friend for constantly worrying about the young woman, and advises Hayami to be glad that Hikari has graduated with distinctions in Business and Economics from one of Tokyo's top universities, and become a *shakaijin*[4] (a social person) and that she has her first job as a management trainee in a large, reputable advertising company. Nakao congratulates her god-daughter Hikari whom she had helped look after on many occasions when Hayami was called away on a business trip. Both women are divorced single mothers, and have a daughter each, though Nakao lives with an elderly mother who adores Hikari as she does her own grand-daughter Niki.

How swiftly time has flown, and how they have aged, Hayami and Nakao sigh. Though relieved to have brought their daughters up well, both women are also anxious about the younger women's future. Could their daughters endure the demands of a professional career as they had? Japanese women are today able to pursue their own dreams and passion as freely as men, but they are unable to realize their dreams in the same way that men could. The corporate workplace is still a male-dominated world in which even men themselves are struggling to survive, remarks the 53-year-old legal director Nakao. Her 51-year-old friend Hayami agrees, and then recalls their own experiences from when they entered the job market upon graduating from university, and developed their respective careers through the difficult post-bubble recession.

Hayami, a senior economist in a large American bank, is unsure if she ought to dissuade Hikari from joining the advertising industry. It is no place for women whose roles are mostly at the lower ranks, as in banking. Hayami has worked for many banks in varying positions – both part-time and full-time – before her capabilities were recognized by her current workplace. Yet, she knows that she has reached the *zecchō* (peak position), from where a woman – especially someone her age – has no opportunity to *kyaria uppu*[5] (career-up). There is no glass ceiling, since everything above is opaque and unknown to women. Hayami is also aware of the excessive workload – for both male and female workers – in the advertising industry, the obligations to drink frequently after work, and the necessity of entertainment activities with clients.

Hikari assures her mother that she would do her best to learn as much as she could in advertising and leave when she is ready to start her own business, and that she would try to not be a victim of *karoshi* (death from overwork), or be pushed around as women have been in the past. After all, a new law[6] to be enacted soon would protect workers from *ijime* (bullying), *pawahara* (power harassment), and various kinds of abusive practices in the workplace. Hayami and Nakao laugh on hearing Hikari's remarks. Then, Nakao advises her god-daughter to not have too much expectations of the new law, which could be yet another vague and ineffective legislation. The Equal Employment Opportunity Law[7] (EEOL), she explains, was enacted in 1986 to supposedly help improve gender equality in the workplace, though the outcomes have been mixed. Women have always been, still are, and would continue to be easy victims in the corporate workplace.

Nakao also expresses her concerns about her own daughter's naiveté and idealism, wondering how well the young woman is surviving in the food and beverage industry, which is as male-dominated and challenging as the advertising world. Niki – a year older than Hikari – has several internships in London and Milan to complete after graduating from a culinary school in Paris on a scholarship granted by her future employer, a restaurant in Tokyo where Niki would work as an apprentice the following year. Niki aspires to have her own restaurant one day which will have an all-female staff, like the sushi restaurant Tsurutokame[8] in Ginza. How Nakao wished her former husband had not misled their only daughter into believing that she could succeed in the same way as he has in the culinary industry. It is tough for a man to become a professional chef, and much tougher for a woman.

The two single mothers agree with each other that young Japanese women today talk incessantly about ideals, dreams, passion, work-life balance, and pursuing *jibunrashī seikatsu* (a lifestyle of their own), that they might be easily disappointed and disillusioned when they experience difficulties in actualizing their goals in white-collar work. Both women had their own dreams too in their younger days, when they also embraced the fervour, ambitions, and desires of having their own *jibunrashī seikatsu* and living fulfilling lives. However, the pressure to marry and give birth was much stronger in the 1980s and 1990s, when a *sengyō shufu*[9] (professional housewife) held a higher status than a *kyaria ūman* (career woman). After their divorce, both Hayami and Nakao have each endured being labelled as *make inu*[10] (loser dog) for having failed to be *ryōsai kenbo*[11] (Good Wives Wise Mothers), or *kyōiku mama*[12] (educating mothers).

'We could at least be complimented for having brought up our daughters well, no?' Hayami says with a chuckle. 'That is impossible, since we cannot celebrate *batsu*[13] (a cross, or being crossed) as a good thing,' Nakao retorts. 'You are *batsu ichi* (one cross, or being crossed once), and I am *batsu ni* (two crosses, or being crossed twice)...we could never be *maru*[14] (round, or whole) again!' Nakao's first marriage to a European lasted two years while she was living in France. She later married a young Japanese man who was training to be a professional chef, and ended her second marriage after six years. Nakao laughs as she recalls her second husband's explanation to the divorce lawyer for the separation:

> My wife is a stubborn and selfish woman who spends most of her time working, and is prouder of being a good lawyer than a good wife or mother.

Nakao had been amused by the ironic comment, since her former husband was typically out of the house every day before sunrise and would not return till after midnight. But to him, it was improper for a married woman with children to be a *hataraku ningen*[15] (working person). Hayami reminds Nakao of how the latter used to be teased – criticized, actually – by friends and colleagues for being among many *kikokushijo*[16] (returnees) who had cultivated the undesirable values, attitudes, and behaviour of westerners from living overseas, and hence failing as a Japanese woman, like all other *konkatsu shippaishita josei* (women who have failed in marriage).

Hikari looks puzzled, and asks why it is always the woman's fault when a marriage breaks down, and why a woman who chooses to not marry is also a failure. Times have changed, and very few of her friends think that a woman's main purpose in life is to support her husband's career and educate her children well. 'If there are still strong views that women should be homemakers, why not ban women from working?' she ponders aloud. After having a good laugh, Hayami says to her daughter:

> If women are banned from working, then your mother would not have been able to support your education. You would also have been married by now and have children of your own (*laughs*). Women need to live, and the government also needs us to keep the economy growing. Employers also get a better deal from hiring women than men, as we are cheaper...

Hikari finds it difficult to believe that women are paid much less than men for doing the same job, and asked the two older women to tell her more about women being contingent workers for the economy. Hayami and Nakao try not to discourage the young woman but to explain a little so that young Hikari could manage her expectations. Women are given opportunities to pursue professional careers when they are needed to meet a labour shortage to keep the economy growing, and are often the first to be fired when there is an economic recession. Even as corporate managers, women are ultimately flexible, non-core players in the office where they are often made to perform tasks that are deemed appropriate for women, and are at times promoted to help improve their employers' corporate profile and public image. More recently, the impending legislation to curb abusive practices such as *ijime* and *pawahara* has given employers more ways to target undesirable or unproductive workers – especially women and older employees – as scapegoats to show that they are complying with the law. Hikari looks shocked when she learns that Nakao had once resigned after being falsely accused of having verbally and emotionally abused a junior employee, but could not receive any help from the government's labour office or a workers' union.

After shifting to more cheerful topics, the conversation that afternoon returns to discussions on the working lives of Japanese women when Hayami and Nakao could not stop laughing at Prime Minister Abe Shinzo's proposed economic initiative – widely referred to as 'womenomics'[17] – to make women 'shine' or become *kagayaku josei* (shiny women). Hikari could not stop giggling when she learns that the English word 'shine' is pronounced in Japanese as *shine*[18] which is the imperative tense of commanding or ordering someone 'to die.' Perhaps it is an intentional pun, they chuckle. Heaving a deep sigh, Hikari says in a pensive and disappointed voice:

> What an irony that Prime Minister Abe's claim to make women 'shine' is pronounced in Japanese as a command for someone to die, *shin e*. Perhaps the pun is intentional? After all, to make women work harder in such a difficult environment is really to force them to die sooner, is it not? Or, perhaps the intention is to make women die as a result of working hard to make their economy shine?
>
> Women are dead in his cabinet. There is only one woman in it.[19] If he does not set an example, how does he expect government offices and companies to promote more women to high positions?

Hikari is referring to Abe's 19-member Cabinet which comprises only one female, Katayama Satsuki, who was appointed as the Minister of Regional Revitalization in October 2018 after a reshuffling. Critics have commented on this poor effort at raising the standing of women in the workplace, despite having first championed the campaign after becoming prime minister in late 2012 (McCurry 2018).

Hayami is proud of her daughter's strong sense of justice, though she is also worried that this might be an impediment to Hikari's ability to adapt to the corporate workplace. Feeling the need to encourage the young woman, Hayami gives the following advice:

> There is no need to be upset. Having more women in an organization does not mean there is gender equality or fairness. Women could be placed merely as props and puppets for display purposes. The

> government and companies will always place their interests ahead of those of citizens and employees.
>
> Just remember that if you have a dream, and are serious about it, you must have the courage and determination to realize it. It is not going to be easy, for women and also for men. To be sure, women have to make more sacrifices and withstand more criticisms than men. Whatever you do, be sure to protect your self-esteem, confidence, and pride. These you can never regain properly if they are lost or destroyed...

The conversation over brunch that afternoon captures the varying difficulties that many women managers have experienced, and are still are experiencing in Japan today. The discussions also highlight how women's already precarious conditions are being exacerbated further both by changes and also the lack of change to state policies and corporate practices over the past decades. All these can be attributed to the persistent treatment of women in Japan as contingent labour for the broader economy (Brinton 1993: 107; Ho 2018: 20), and their value as a pool of 'under-utilized,' 'cheap,' and 'expendable resource' to be utilized to suit the country's changing political agendas and economic needs (Waswo 1996: 154). Women have been mobilized for the nation's modernization programme during the Meiji era, for the postwar reconstruction of the economy, to meet the labour shortage during the rapid economic expansion during the bubble decade, and again to fill gaps in the white-collar workforce in post-bubble Japan. The significance of women as economic tools is thus not new at all. It has only taken on the new, modern business rhetoric of womenomics.

At the same time, the socio-cultural perceptions of women and expectations of their roles in Japanese society have also remained relatively unchanged. The old Meiji feminine ideal of *ryōsai kenbo* (Good Wives Wise Mothers) has also merely shifted rhetorically to the postwar model of *sengyō shufu* (professional or full-time housewives) to continuously designate women's rightful place in society to their domestic roles as wife, mother, and caregiver (Uno 1993: 301; White 2002: 126; Yoda 2006: 247). The socio-historical construction of femininity too is aimed at benefitting the economy. Women marry and give birth to provide a steady stream of workers for the economy; they receive education to train a more competent future labour force; and women's role in caring for the elderly and other members of the family helps alleviate the state's burden of providing welfare.

This accounts for why women have always occupied a marginal position in the workforce, where their careers are not taken seriously as those of their male counterparts. This also explains why the state persistently ignores many signs of drastic demographic shifts to improve work conditions for women by implementing policies without adequate monitoring, and hence allows employers to continuously exploit this vulnerable category of the country's population. As the pervasive influence of neoliberal capitalism transforms the work environment and erodes employees' sense of job security for both men and women, this worsens the precarious conditions and experiences of women as the dominant non-core, peripheral players in the corporate workplace.

The social reproduction of precarity for women managers

This book is about how women manage the varying difficult social and economic conditions that they encounter as corporate managers in post-bubble Japan. It examines how women managers struggle in an increasingly flexible work environment and a persistently male-dominated society, and how their position of marginality and vulnerability is continuously exploited and exacerbated by state policies and corporate practices. I have previously documented the innovative ways in which 27 women managers in Tokyo mobilize their friendship as a strategic site to mitigate the disappointments in their working lives, and conceptualize new understandings of independence and equality (Ho 2012b, 2018). This book expands on these works by examining the broader structural conditions that shape the experiences of 160 women in supervisory and managerial positions across Japan. More specifically, it analyses how precarity is produced, reinforced, and perpetuated by continuities and discontinuities in shifting structural processes that generate and perpetuate the experiences of angst, anxiety, frustrations, disillusionment, and insecurity for this particular segment of the population. By precarity, I refer to the 'structure of daily life' that entails the incessant concerns about work performance, job security, and the sustainability of economic life (McCormack and Salmenniemi 2017: 4). I also follow Flavia Cangià (2018: 10–1) in understanding precarity as the subjective experiences of individuals that have been shaped and exacerbated by unequal power relations through processes of change to the broader political, economic, and socio-cultural environments.

Despite a phenomenal increase in the number of white-collar female workers in Japan over the past few decades, their lives and experiences still remain under-studied, and those of women in managerial positions are understood even less. Studies on precarious labour and experiences of precarity in Japan have focused mostly on the struggles of women and youths who are in irregular employment and informal jobs (Allison 2012; Brinton 2011; Roberts 1994; Slater 2010). The silence in scholarly literature on Japan reflects a similar lack of attention paid by the broader anthropological scholarship to the predicaments of corporate managers and women managers.

Scholarship on precarity and precariousness has exploded over the years to discuss the implications of the neoliberal flexible work regime on income stability and job security of workers (Kalleberg and Vallas 2018; Vosko 2011). Since Pierre Bourdieu's study of working class families in the 1960s and the social problem of the *précarité* (insecurity) as the fundamental dimension of the experience of work, the term precarity has been widely used in association with 'employment that is uncertain, unpredictable, and risky'

(Kalleberg 2009: 2). Concerns about how the marginalization and exclusion of workers have increased their vulnerability and insecurity have spawned many works on the abject conditions of individuals – both men and women – in irregular work, youth employment, and seasonal migrant jobs that come with low wages, no minimum wage protection, short contractual terms, and negligible benefits (Biehl 2016; Campbell 2016; Curtin and Sanson 2016; Ehrenreich and Hochschild 2002; Kretsos 2011; Lan 2002; Millar 2014; Parreñas 2002; Vosko 2000).

In recent years, a growing body of literature has emerged to explore the precarious situations of white-collar workers with the rising incidence of flexible work that render their jobs meaningless and their struggles futile (De Certeau 1984; Sennett 2000). There are also studies on the production of 'precarious elites' (Thorkelson 2016: 483), due to a 'jarring disconnect' between graduate education and the realities of the flexible job market in academia (Muehlebach 2012: 305), and of countless 'graduates with no future,' such as those who work as adjunct lecturers working in universities (Bousquet 2002; Žižek 2012).

While there is a wide consensus on the pervasive and adverse influence of the neoliberal transformations of work on individuals' experiences in diverse forms of employment, scholarship has paid extensive attention to the precarious conditions of workers at the lower strata of society and the bottom of the employment system. There is a paucity of data on how the work conditions of individuals in managerial positions and certain professions – especially those of women's – are equally exposed to the same processes of change to the work environment as irregular workers, and share similar experiences of anxiety and insecurity due to a growing lack of secure work-based identity.

This silence in scholarship is perhaps due to varying difficulties of access that scholars may encounter to workers who are generally perceived as occupying 'privileged' positions in the job market. More likely, it is due to perceptions of corporate managers and various professionals as 'privileged' individuals whose work situation is more secure given their relatively high incomes when compared to the situations faced by irregular and informal workers. In reality, working as corporate managers is no longer a stable or secure job in today's environment of neoliberal capitalism, where corporations are relentlessly reducing staff costs as a key strategic means of managing profitability, and utilizing modern management methods of disciplining permanent employees (Gagné 2018: 72). As the old Japanese system of employment – based on the three pillars of lifetime employment, seniority wages, and enterprise unionism – gave way to new international styles of business and management based on meritocracy and individual performance, the corporate work environment gradually became more company-centred, rendering the daily lives of employees more susceptible to policies and practices of individual corporations (Hall and Soskice 2001: 6; Keizer 2010: 7).

As Nancy Ettlinger (2007: 322) remarks, precarity 'spares no one, haunting even privileged persons.' Yet, Laura Nader (1972: 304) points out that there is the problem of double standard of 'studying up' and 'studying down' in scholarly approach to analyzing the lives of subjects. As Eli Thorkelson (2016: 481) also notes, anthropologists tend to shy away from 'studying up' for reasons which include their unwillingness to be intimidated by 'privileged' individuals, whereas 'studying down' places them in a position of authority over the subjects of their inquiry. But as Sherry B. Ortner (1998: 428) demonstrates in her study of a distinct cohort of hippies and yuppies in the US known as Generation X, anxieties and feelings of insecurity are experienced and dealt with in diverse ways by individuals of different categories of gender, class, and social status. Exploring how a certain category of a population encounters the same difficult economic conditions as others deepens our understanding of how this group of individuals also manage problematic social conditions that may be shared by others (Ibid.: 418). Examining the lives of corporate managers and other 'privileged individuals' need not be seen as a form 'studying up,' though omitting their voices and lived experiences would impoverish our understanding of the richness and complexities of social reality which comprises the experiences of individuals of diverse occupations and professions.

Precarity is the predominant experiential dimension of the crisis in today's society of flexible work that has evolved since the 1980s with widespread implementations of neoliberal policies by many states to achieve political control and economic benefits (Harvey 1989). This has resulted in a disintegration of stable societal bonds, destruction of occupational identities, a weakening of collective representative powers to provide individuals with adequate protection against exploitation, and an intense disciplining of personal values to suit the goals of corporations, individuals higher up the corporate ladder experience just as much economic uncertainty and existential angst (Chauvière and Mick 2011; Klikauer 2015). Understanding how the lives of corporate managers and their experiences in particular localities would shed fresh insights into the specific the ways in which shifts in the adaptation of neoliberal tools by agents of power have shaped the emergence of new opportunities and challenges for an under-documented category of the working population.

Moreover, the corporate workplace is not a neutral or safe space, but a 'battleground infused with contradictions and conflicts,' and with territorial boundaries carefully drawn to divide people (Skachkova 2007: 705). Given that women managers are a small minority and are treated as 'outsiders' in the corporate workplace, they often experience 'a sense of being out of place, out of sorts, disconnected' (Allison 2013: 14), and hence are more vulnerable and insecure to be in a place where they do not belong (Hinkson 2017). This is the case in Japan, where women managers are still a small minority whose works are persistently under-valued and unvalued both by the state and employers (Osawa 2005; Steinhoff and Tanaka 1993; Yuasa 2005), but are valued primarily for being cheap resource (Brinton 1993; Ho 2018; Lam 1993). It is the historically consistent treatment of women as an economic tool by the Japanese government and employers that has produced, reproduced, and perpetuated the precarious conditions that women managers are in.

Precarity cannot be understood as an ahistorical unidimensional notion (Matos 2019: 16), but as a historical and multi-faceted dynamic that gradually structures and permeates every aspect of an individual life. As Nader (1997: 721–2) describes cultures as 'historical ideas' that are controlled by structural processes which gain their power incrementally over time, the tensions and conflicts that are 'experienced and lived' are also shaped by processes of change over time for a particular category of people based on their social position and status in a given society (Millar 2014: 35).

The problem of womenomics as always

In 2014, one year after Prime Minister Abe announced his wide-ranging fiscal and labour reforms – which is widely known today as 'Abenomics' – his government released a special issue of the quarterly bulletin *We Are Tomodachi* (We Are Friends) called 'Womenomics' to declare the need for women to 'play an increasingly active role in Japan' (JapanGov 2014: 16). An article in the bulletin also states that the government is pushing forward various measures to 'increase the percentage of women in leadership position to 30 per cent,' and that the country 'is now making rapid progress toward turning those words into reality by creating a Japan where women can shine' (Ibid.: 18).

Three years later, an article entitled 'Toward a Society Where All Women Shine'[20] in the same quarterly bulletin cites the Organisation for Economic Co-operation and Development (OECD) as reporting that 'the labour force participation rate for Japanese women aged 25–64 has reached 71.1 per cent, surpassing the figure of 69.9% for the United States' (JapanGov 2017: 24). While the article acknowledges 'the glass ceiling that hinders women from rising to executive positions continues to be an issue in Japan,' the government is said to have taken measures 'to address this issue, with a focus on increasing the numbers of women in executive posts' (Ibid.). One such measure was a five-day intensive Executive Program for Women Leaders participated by 66 high-ranking women managers from leading companies in Japan, who were 'motivated by Prime Minister Abe's address at the closing reception' as 'a sign of government support for their career goals' (Ibid.: 25). The article then concludes that '[S]ince 60 companies sent managers to this program, we should soon see women sitting on 60 corporate boards' (Ibid.).

Japan's female workforce participation has risen significantly over the past decades, though the government's official statistics showed the rate to be 51.1 per cent for women in 2017, in contrast to 70.5 per cent for men (SHJ 2018: 122). The fact that a 'glass ceiling' still poses difficulties for women to ascend the corporate ladder is true. The article cites a survey conducted by data services company Toyo Keizai as showing that the total of 1,400 female board members in the country accounted for only 3.5 per cent of all corporate board memberships of the country (JapanGov 2017: 25). Not only is the figure far beneath the 30-per cent target proclaimed by Abe's government three years earlier, but it has also not risen much since 2017. According to a research report issued by the American investment bank Goldman Sachs, female participation in corporate board membership stands at approximately 5.3 per cent in 2019.

Then, there is the question of how many female board members have real executive powers to actively participate in and influence high-level corporate decisions as their male counterparts, and how many are nominal executives appointed as a cosmetic arrangement to enhance the profile of a company's board and its corporate image. A similar question could be raised about the Japanese government's statement that 'we should soon see women sitting on 60 corporate boards' (JapanGov 2017: 25), given these 60 women managers had been sent by their employers to participate in the state-funded training programme at the request of the government to illustrate the 'success' of Abe's womenomics. Several, if not all, of the appointments could be cosmetically arranged, since there are benefits to be gained from being 'women-friendly companies,' which are entitled to receiving various incentives including subsidies, tax reductions, awards, and public praise by the government (MOFA 2015: 4).

Yakuin (corporate board of directors) has never been a female realm. Japan historically ranks at the bottom among OECD countries in female representation in leadership and managerial positions in both the public and private sectors (Matsui et al. 2019: 23). As of September 2019, Abe's own Cabinet comprises only two female ministers.[21] Most large Japanese corporations also have very few female board members. Sumitomo Mitsui Financial Group[22] has only one female as 'outside director' among a total of nine external members, and none from within the company. Mitsubishi UFJ[23] too does not appoint any female employee on its board, as all three female board members are from 'outside.' Softbank Group[24] has several non-Japanese on its board but there is no female. As for cosmetic group Shiseido,[25] five out of 11 members of the board are female, though four are external members. Despite being perceived as among the most progressive Japanese companies, the country's two largest advertising conglomerates Dentsu and Hakuhodo also do not have female representation. The two female members on Dentsu's board of 12 are non-executive directors from 'outside' the company, while Hakuhodo's 13-member board has no female. There is clearly a disjuncture between state rhetoric and reality.

Furthermore, middle to lower management too appears to be male-dominated spaces. Official statistics compiled by the Ministry of Health, Labour and Welfare (MHLW) indicate – though without providing details on the types of work – that 13.2 per cent of the country's 'administrative and managerial workers' in 2017 were female, while 86.8 per cent were male

(SHJ 2018: 128). The figure does not seem to have changed much since. It is estimated that female executives still account for approximately 14 per cent of all managerial positions in the country in 2019 (Matsui et al. 2019: 22), a meagre increase from a previous estimate of 10 per cent in 2010 (Matsui et al. 2010: 18). Women managers are a small minority in Japan still, despite a significant increase in white-collar female workers over the past five decades. As shown in Table 1.1, Japan's white-collar labour force doubled in size from 28.8 million in 1965 to 56.4 million in 2015, but the number of women working as company employees nearly tripled from 9.1 million in 1965 to 24.7 million in 2015 (JILPT 2017: 20–1).

Indeed, there have been improved opportunities for women to gain greater access to salaried work and even improve their career prospects (Blind and Mandach 2015: 54). However, since most of their subordinates, peers, and superiors are Japanese, and higher levels of management are still occupied by men, female corporate managers are still to deal with certain challenges pertaining to prevailing gender perceptions and cultural practices. The persistently gendered and increasingly demanding work environments have led many female corporate workers to gradually leave the job market or devise strategies to maintain lasting economic stability (Nemoto 2013: 513–4; Roberts 2011: 573). In addition, a growing number of women has over the years shied away from Japanese employers and joined foreign corporations, in the hope of being better recognized for their capabilities, of gaining favourable prospects for advancing their careers, and having greater exposure to international business practices (Ho 2018: 69).

It is also important to note that only approximately 44.5 per cent of all white-collar female workers are regular employees, while 78 per cent of all male employees are regular workers (see Table 1.2 for figures in 2017). Clearly, women's lower participation in regular corporate employment explains why women are not well represented in supervisory or managerial positions, though the reason for the lower number of regular female employees

Table 1.1 Company employees by gender from 1965 to 2015 (*in millions*)

Year	*Total in employment*	*Male*	*Female*	*Total employees*	*Male*	*Female*	*% of total employees*	
							Male	*Female*
1965	47.3	28.5	18.8	28.8	19.6	9.1	68.3	31.7
1970	50.9	30.9	20.0	33.1	22.1	11.0	66.8	33.2
1980	55.4	33.9	21.4	39.7	26.2	13.5	65.9	34.1
1990	62.5	37.1	25.4	48.4	30.0	18.3	62.1	37.9
2000	64.5	38.2	26.3	53.6	32.2	21.4	60.0	40.0
2010	62.6	36.2	26.4	54.6	31.3	23.3	57.3	42.6
2015	63.8	36.2	27.5	56.4	31.7	24.7	56.1	43.9

Source: The Japan Institute of Policy and Training (2018: 20–1).

suggests that there is a stronger proclivity among employers to hire women as cheaper workers on short-term contracts of employment. This applies to regular female workers as well. As statistics also show, regular female workers are paid approximately 72 per cent of the average annual salary of their male counterparts, and receive less than 60 per cent of the total annual bonuses that Japanese men are paid (JILPT 2017: 47).

It is evident from the figures shown earlier that while women's labour contributions are important to the country's workforce, they are valued for being a pool of economical resources. Whether it is called womenomics or given another name, the trend of utilizing women primarily – if not solely – for the purpose of their contributions to the economy is hardly new, as mentioned before. Women have historically been utilized as contingent labour for the country's economic programmes. The phenomenal increase in the number of management-track careers was offered to women during the 1990s, when economic growth reached its peak and turned Japan into the world's second largest economy after the US. Japan's rapidly growing retail and financial services sectors were experiencing a labour shortage, and demanded a larger female workforce to serve the industries' expanding female customer base. Later, white-collar female workers were once again preferred by employers as cheap resources during the prolonged economic recession after the demise of the country's bubble economy. The country's white-collar male workforce has been shrinking over the past two decades, as more employers replace permanent jobs with short-term, temporary positions in the increasingly flexible post-bubble work environment. As shown in Table 1.1, the total number of male employees dropped from 32.3 million in 2000 to 31.7 million in 2015, while the country's total white-collar female workforce expanded from 21.4 million to 24.7 million over the same period (JILPT 2017: 20–1). What the Japanese government's womenomics agenda seems to have done, in terms of creating more white-collar work opportunities for women, is the expansion of the country's cheap, flexible, and insecure workforce.

What is perhaps different, new, and potentially more dangerous about womenomics as an ideological tool is that it has gained greater legitimacy as a lauded initiative in modern business and state governance that intensifies the justification of state policies and corporate practices in extracting more value out of the country's female workforce by promoting more women to

Table 1.2 Company employees by gender in 2017 (*in millions*)

	Total employees	*Regular*	*% of total employed*	*Irregular*	*% of total employed*
	54.6	34.2	*62.7*	20.4	*37.3*
Male	29.6	23.1	*78.1*	6.5	*21.9*
Female	25.0	11.1	*44.5*	13.9	*55.5*

Source: Statistical Handbook of Japan (2018: 129).

supervisory and managerial positions, but with controls in place to keep the cost of the female corporate management workforce low, coupled with insufficient measures to improve on their working conditions. Given the persistent neglect on the part of the state to resolve many past and current problems, more difficulties have emerged to increase women's vulnerability in the corporate workplace, undermine the sustainability of their economic life, exacerbate their job insecurity, and hence further aggravate their precarious conditions. The playing field has never been a levelled one for the two sexes. The increasingly flexible work environment may have generated similar challenges for men and women in Japan, but women's marginal place in Japanese society and their role as non-core players in corporate workplace expose them to further difficulties and threats that relate to the problem of their being 'female,' which are not shared by their male counterparts.

With perceptions of gender remaining conservative and unchanged, employers will continue to not take women's professional careers seriously and also to limit women's career opportunities. As employers continue to adopt newer and more modern business methods to promote managerialism and entrepreneurialism, female managers will experience more difficulties in their work and face greater risks in the workplace. And as a new legislation offers employers with new and more extensive justifications to threaten and exploit employees to show their compliance with curbing workplace bullying and power harassment, women as the 'weaker sex' in the office will be further exposed to risks of being victimized as perpetrators. Given the historically weak voice that labour unions in Japan have, women managers – as well as other employees – lack the ability to seek redress through collective representations from unfair and abusive practices at work. Many women managers are already experiencing a wide range of stresses and conflicts that have emerged over the past decades, and are questioning the futility and meaninglessness of being *kanrisha* (a manager). Indeed, women have made substantial inroads into the labour market in Japan to gain regular employment and real wage enhancement (Blind and Mandach 2015: 68–9), but their improved situation has also aggravated their precarious conditions with serious long-term re-ramifications on their physical, emotional, and mental health, as well as on aspects of their personal, family, and professional lives.

This study

This book presents the narratives of many women managers in Japan from a total of 160 subjects, and offers insights into their lived experiences as female corporate managers in a rapidly changing and increasingly challenging work environment in post-bubble Japan.

In discussing the difficulties presented by state policies and corporate practices, the details might depict the working lives of women managers in Japan in a negative and gloomy light. It is not the intention of this book to highlight only the problems and contradictions, as many of my informants have benefitted significantly from improvements made to various policies and practices, and developed life trajectories that are radically different from those of women of previous generations.

Indeed, an increasing number of women have experienced enhanced economic capital that permits them to have *jibunrashī seikatsu* and find fulfilment in ways that their mothers could only imagine but not realize. Nonetheless, the opportunities and gains that these women have experienced have not come without difficulties and sacrifices. The intention of this book is to draw attention to the various critical problems relating to state policies and corporate practices that have persisted, and also new ones that have emerged, which could have been better managed, reduced, or eradicated in order to effect positive change to the work environment amidst radical change, but they have instead posed further contradictions and ambivalences in the lives of many women managers in Japan.

The fieldwork

The data for this book come from various phases of fieldwork which began in January 2002. My fieldwork comprises three long and many short stays in Japan. The first of the three length phases was an eight-month period from January to September 2002, when I was working as Vice President in an international, multimedia conglomerate and was on a business assignment to supervise the restructuring of the company's Tokyo-based subsidiary. During the eight months, I spent many evenings out drinking with colleagues and business associates, as well as meeting their friends and acquaintances. Since my job involved the re-allocation and recruitment of employees, I spent a considerable amount of time interviewing white-collar workers in supervisory and managerial positions. The detailed notes I kept were to later become valuable data for my research.

I returned to Tokyo in March 2003, and spent two years conducting research on various aspects of the lives of Japanese women as graduate students until June 2005. My next field trip was a nine-month period in Tokyo from March 2007 till January 2008, when I returned again to gather data for my doctoral study of women managers in Japan. I made more than 25 short field trips – of one-week to two-month durations each – in between the three intensive phases mentioned earlier, and after January 2008 till today. I communicate frequently with many informants while I am not in Japan, via social media, text messages, and telephone calls. I have travelled with many of them – in small groups of three to five – on short holidays to various places in Asia, Australia, Europe, and North America. Many women have also visited me outside Japan – in England, Hong Kong, Seoul, and Singapore – during their business trips or while on holiday with their family.

I have interviewed more than 200 white-collar workers of various ranks and positions, both male and female, across many cities in Japan for various research projects. This book is based on the field data gathered from unstructured interviews with 160 women in supervisory and managerial positions, and from participant-observations of the activities. It also draws on additional field data collected from interviews with 40 male managers and corporate executives of 30 Japanese companies from across the country. What began as a snowballing sampling method of data-gathering gradually became webs of many informal, though strong, networks of women with professional careers across many cities in Japan. Having known many of my informants for nearly two decades, I am a frequent guest at many homes, and have come to learn many aspects of the women's professional, personal, and family lives.

Issues from the field

The field data have been enlightening, though the process of gathering has not been an easy one. Having worked as a corporate executive, I was able to share my own work-related experiences with my subjects and relate to the different encounters of many. Some women readily recounted their experiences to me in the presence of a mutual acquaintance or friend, though more than half of my 160 informants were more willing to give detailed accounts of their experiences when we talked on a one-to-one basis. Still, it was difficult for many women to express their feelings of disappointment, anger, frustrations, humiliation, and disillusionment relating to their jobs. It was much harder for them to share their experiences of unfair or abusive treatment. Most of my informants gradually felt comfortable to open up only after the second or third meeting with me. Many women found – and still find – it embarrassing as highly educated and professionally qualified corporate executives discuss their work-related difficulties, for fear that they would be laughed at for being weak, incapable, or incompetent. However, coping with how they are perceived by others has been as challenging as managing their own-image. A considerably large number of my subjects say that their friends or family members have expressed disbelief on hearing the women's experiences and grievances. Some have been told that they are petty or difficult individuals who are constantly complaining, whining, and moaning. Many hence prefer to keep their work problems to themselves, and would share them only with like-minded friends, particularly those who are also career women (Ho 2018: 46–76).

Granted, it is not uncommon for Japanese men to avoid work talk in the home or with general friends, due to reasons given by white-collar female workers discussed earlier. Male office workers too are afraid to be perceived as weak, incapable, or incompetent, qualities which are not regarded as masculine. However, the experiences of their female counterparts are confouned by the added problem of being 'women.' Many of my informants who are single have struggled with remarks by others for being self-centred and stubborn, and some have been advised to get married so that they would not have to deal with the problems of having a professional career. While those who are married have also been described as self-centred and stubborn, many women's difficulties in the office were attributed to their inability to cope with the dual demands of career and family. 'You would be happier if you were to quit working and be a full-time mother' was a phrase that married women have heard after sharing their work-related problems with friends and family members. These remarks and advice are not unfamiliar to those who are divorced, who are often deemed as having prioritized career over family, and hence failed in their marriage for being negligent wives and irresponsible mothers. Despite the wide-ranging difficulties that white-collar workers in Japan have to cope with, the experiences of many female corporate executives seem to be readily attributed to their problem of being 'women,' and less to the persistent structural challenges posed by state policies and corporate practices.

The subjects

The 160 women in supervisory and managerial positions interviewed for this book are aged between 25 and 65 years. Of these, approximately 15 per cent are aged 25–35 years, while 36 per cent are in the 36–45 age group, with 39 per cent aged 46–55 years, and 10 per cent are above 55 years of age (see Table 1.3). The majority of my informants are aged between 35 and 55 years, due largely to the access that I have gained to women managers over a prolonged period of fieldwork spanning from 2002 when I began this research. Studying women belonging to this age group enables me to track the upturns and downturns in their career through the many neoliberal changes that have taken place in state policies and the corporate workplace.

In terms of marital status, one-third of the women are single, while another one-third are married, and the remaining one-third divorced (as shown in Table 1.4). While the sample size is too small to indicate if marriage poses a hindrance to their pursuit of a professional career, the fact that two-thirds of my informants are single and divorced might suggest that many women choose or find it possible to work outside of wedlock. A clearer indication perhaps lies in the high number of married and divorced women with no children (see Table 1.5). Only 24 out of 67 women who are married have children, while 43 do not. Among the 50 women who are divorced, more than half or 33 have no children, while 17 are divorced single mothers. Moreover, all but six of the 41 women who are mothers have only one child. The figures – which are limited only to this study – highlight the difficulties posed by childbirth and child-rearing to the women's career pursuits than the demands of marriage (Roberts 2011: 575).

The women's educational backgrounds also show the considerable demands exerted on them to upgrade themselves by acquiring professional

Table 1.3 Age profiles of research subjects (total of 160)

Age	*Number*	*Percentage of total*
25–35 years	24	*15*
36–45 years	58	*36*
46–55 years	62	*39*
56–65 years	16	*10*
	160	

Table 1.4 Marital status of research subjects (total of 160)

Status	*Number*	*% of total*	*With children*	*No children*
Single	43	*27*		
Married	67	*42*	24	43
Divorced	50	*31*	17	33
	160			

Table 1.5 Current employers of research subjects by company type and size (total of 160)

Company type	*Number of research subjects*	*Small*	*Medium*	*Large*	*% of total*
		(less than 50 employees)	*(50–250 employees)*	*(more than 250 employees)*	
Japanese	68	26	34	8	*43*
Foreign	92	18	56	18	*57*
	160	*32%*	*53%*	*15%*	

Note: The company sizes are based on definitions by the Organisation for Economic Co-operation and Development (OECD).

qualifications. All but five women are university graduates. Nearly 110 women have acquired further academic and professional qualifications, which include Master's degree in Business Administration (MBA), Certified Public Accountant (CPA), Chartered Financial Analyst (CFA), and post-graduate diplomas in fields related to their respective lines of work. However, almost all my informants work in low and mid-levels of management. While nine are technically in upper management – holding job titles such as director and vice president – all of them say that they have little or no executive powers, and are not active in important decision-making activities of their respective places of work.

In terms of their employers, more women seem to have developed their careers in foreign companies than in Japanese firms. As shown in Table 1.5, two-fifths of my subjects work for Japanese companies, while the other three-fifths are employees of foreign corporations. The number who works in small-sized Japanese businesses amounts to 26, outnumbering 18 employees of small non-Japanese firms. However, only eight women are managers in large Japanese corporations, in contrast to 18 women in large foreign companies. Meanwhile, more than half of the 160 women under study are hired in medium-sized companies, while another one-third work for small enterprises. Based on my sample, it appears that more Japanese women have been are able to pursue a professional career in medium- to large-sized foreign companies than in Japanese corporations.

More importantly, the majority of the women under study hold supervisory or managerial positions in typically 'feminine types of work' (Lam 1993: 198), such as finance, corporate communications, customer service, human resource management, marketing, office administration, public relations, tax accounting, and treasury. These are back-office, non-profit generating divisions which are historically female domains, and lower in status than the types of work that Japanese men do. Only 17 out of my 160 informants are in predominantly male lines of work, which comprise business development, product design, sales, and the legal department. Also, nearly all of my informants are employed in the retail, financial services, and wholesale industries which are also 'traditionally female-intensive sectors' (Ibid.). The opportunities that presented an unprecedented number of Japanese women to pursue management-track careers during the bubble decade in the 1980s remain little changed. Even today, a gender divide still exists in many companies, where women are yet to make significant inroads into taking up positions in important corporate divisions that are of higher status.

The aforementioned patterns are also reflected in the profiles of the subjects discussed in this book (see *Appendix*). How women managers in Japan cope with their daily work lives under such circumstances will be elucidated in greater detail in subsequent chapters.

The chapters

So far, this chapter has laid out the scope and significance of the issues to be elaborated in this book. It contends that the persistent deployment of women as a pool of cheap, expendable resource by the Japanese state and employers is posing conflicts and contradictions in the lives of women working as corporate managers. This chapter also argues that the intensified push for womenomics by the government would aggravate the precarious conditions that women managers are already experiencing.

Chapter 2 examines the proliferation of negative discourses on and portrayals of women with professional careers in the local popular media since the 1980s as a reflection of how they are perceived in the broader Japanese society. It scrutinizes many women's narratives on the range of difficulties they have encountered, and are still encountering, in managing meaningful and coherent self-identities.

Chapter 3 analyses the changing significance of after-work drinking for white-collar workers and the enactment of culturally constituted gender roles as some of the strategies for women managers to manage the challenges they experience in their relations with subordinates, peers, and superiors. As *tenshoku* (job-changing) replaces permanent employment to become the dominant work norm in post-bubble Japan, the flexible work environment leads to weaker and disharmonious relations among employees, and increases the importance of drinking among co-workers for corporate managers as a necessary means of stabilizing relations with subordinates in order to protect their jobs.

Chapter 4 takes a closer look at women's struggles within the office as corporate executives and the rise of modern management methods of managerialism in post-bubble Japan. It discusses how a loophole in Japan's antiquated labour laws permits employers to utilize *nabakari kanrishoku* (nominal management) as a useful tool to promote employees to managerial positions for enhancing their corporate image, and hence reinforces women's role as non-core players in the corporate workplace.

The Japanese state's ambivalent role is examined in Chapter 5. Close attention is paid to analysing the ineffectiveness of legislations implemented by the MHLW. More specifically, the chapter will explain how the introduction of a new legislation to supposedly curb *ijime* (workplace bullying) and *pawahara* (power harassment) ironically presents employers with new justifications to further exacerbate the precarious conditions of white-collar female workers. This chapter also includes discussions on the historically weak position of labour unions and their inability to provide adequate supportive structures and power of collective representations for workers to seek redress for unjust and unfair treatment in the workplace.

Chapter 6 details the narratives and experiences of a young female management trainee (mentioned in Chapter 1) as a way of projecting into the future what the work environment in Japan would be like for younger generations of women managers, given the existing range of structural problems that have been discussed throughout this book.

Notes

1 Place names and all Japanese terms that are commonly used in English – such as Tokyo, Osaka, and Kyoto – are not italicized or written with diacritical markings. All other Japanese words are italicized or written with appropriate diacritical markings when they occur, such as *sararīman* and *izakaya*.

2 All names mentioned are pseudonyms, for the purpose of protecting the identities of my informants. Japanese names are arranged by the family name first, followed by the first name. See ***Appendix*** for details on all informants' profiles.

3 I am using the younger Hayami's first name Hikari to avoid confusion with references to her mother.

4 The term *sararīman* describes someone who has become a member of society after gaining economic independence by securing employment. For future reference, all Japanese words are transliterated or romanized according to the Kenkyūsha's New Japanese-English Dictionary.

5 The term means to advance one's career in gaining a higher position in a company.
6 The Cabinet in March 2019 had approved legal revisions to ban workplace harassment by requiring companies to prevent abuses of power or bullying, as part of a bundle of bills aimed at promoting the advancement of working women at smaller firms. These legal changes proposed by the Ministry of Labour, Health and Welfare (MHLW) may take effect in 2020 if passed by the parliament known as the Diet in 2019 (Kyodo 2019).
7 The Japanese government implemented the EEOL in 1986 primarily in recognition of the need to fully utilize the female work force to meet a projected labour shortage due to declining birth rates and a rapidly ageing population. However, the legislation has been criticized for its ineffectiveness by many, given the lack of punitive measures for employers who did not comply in practice. See detailed discussions in Chapter 2.
8 Tsurutokame, which was opened in 2016, is a sushi restaurant run by an all-female staff, though it is owned by Mikuni Osamu and his wife Harumi.
9 The postwar female ideal of the *sengyō shufu* was that of a full-time housewife who devotes all time and energy to child-bearing, child-rearing, and care-giving.
10 See detailed discussions on *make inu* in Chapter 2.
11 The Confucian female ideal *ryōsai kenbo* was institutionalized by the Meiji government to implement a sexual division of labour which assigns women's rightful place in Japanese society to the domestic realm.
12 Mothers, especially full-time housewives, are heavily involved in their children's education and school activities, and are hence often referred to as 'educating mothers.'
13 The term *batsu* means 'a cross' to describe a woman who has failed in her marriage. Once divorced, she is given 'one cross' and is thus referred to as *batsu ichi* (*ichi* means 'one'). If divorced twice, she is described as having *batsu ni* or 'two crosses' (*ni* means 'two'). Despite increasing incidences of divorce (*rikon*) in Japan, there still exist perceptions of divorced women as having 'failed' in their marriage, and are hence described in terms of a cross (Alexy 2011: 902).
14 The metaphor of a *maru* ('circle' or 'round') in the context of a woman's marital status refers to the wholeness or completeness a woman's being, that is, her life is in keeping with prevailing gender expectations in playing her role as wife and perhaps also as mother.
15 This term is often used to describe people who are devoted to their work.
16 The term is used to refer to Japanese people who have returned to Japan after growing up overseas.
17 Expanding the country's female workforce and promoting women to managerial positions are a part of Abe's long-term economic growth strategy which his government refers to as 'Abenomics.'
18 The Japanese word *shin e* is the imperative form of the verb *shinu*, which means 'to die.'
19 Prime Minister Abe Shinzo's 19-member cabinet comprises one female Katayama Satsuki, who was appointed as the Minister of Regional Revitalization in October 2018 after a reshuffling. Critics have commented on this poor effort at raising the standing of women in the workplace, despite having first championed the campaign after becoming prime minister in late 2012 (McCurry 3 October 2018).
20 This reiterates Abe's plan to 'Create a Society in which Women Shine' (*josei ga kagayaku shakai wo tsukuru*).
21 Takaichi Sanae – Minister for Internal Affairs and Communications, and Minister of State for the Social Security and Tax Number System – was the only

female in Abe's Cabinet until a reshuffling in September 2019. A second female member Hashimoto Seiko was named the Minister for the Tokyo Olympic and Paralympic Games, Minister in charge of Women's Empowerment, and Minister of State for Gender Equality. For more information, see URL at https://japan.kantei.go.jp/98_abe/meibo/daijin/index_e.html

22 More information can be found on Sumitomo Mitsui's URL: www.smfg.co.jp/english/company/info/officer.html

23 More information can be found on Mitsubishi UFJ's URL: www.mufg.jp/english/profile/overview/management/people/#jump01

24 Softbank: https://group.softbank/en/corp/about/officer/

25 More information can be found on Shiseido's website URL: www.shiseidogroup.com/company/board/

2 In the media

As flowers, parasites, loser dogs, and demons

I have not seen Kishida Kiyoko for nearly two years before we eventually met one Sunday in June 2019. She had also invited with several acquaintances Sawabe Sayori, Namiki Naomi, and Takagi Tomoe to brunch at an old family-run *sobaya-san* (Japanese restaurant serving noodles made from buckwheat) in Tokyo district of Kanda. Kishida and Sawabe had once worked together for the same employer during the early 2000s, though they have also not seen much of each other over the past years. The 46-year-old Kishida has been busy since being promoted to deputy head of corporate communications in the mid-sized American consultancy firm, while Sawabe had resigned to join an Italian fashion distributor as manager of merchandising. The two women would meet once in a while, whenever the 45-year-old Sawabe is not on a business trip, or could find time away from her commitments as a divorced single mother. Kishida has mentioned to me on several occasions that Sawabe has long wanted to meet this anthropologist whom she heard has been studying the lives of women managers in Japan. But our schedules have not permitted us to meet till that morning. Kishida too often travels for work and leisure, and would devote whatever little free time she has to calligraphy and watercolour painting, activities that would have been impossible if she was married and had children to look after. Meanwhile, Kishida too has been looking forward to meeting Namiki, Sawabe's university peer whom the latter often describes as someone with the rare audacity and tenacity to stand up against unfairness and injustice in the workplace. Until that Sunday, Sawabe and Namiki have not seen each other much after an alumni gathering a decade following their graduation from the University of Tokyo. On meeting Namiki, Sawabe instantly realizes that she remembers having read media coverage on Namiki's success in fighting a lengthy legal battle with her former employer for unfair dismissal. The Sunday brunch is also the first time that Sawabe gets to meet Takagi, a 39-year-old public relations manager whom Kishida has talked so much about, for being an unusually supportive boss and rare mentor to junior workers.

There is much excitement as the women exchange introductions and their experiences. As we make our way into the desserts, the conversation turns to the third season of the television drama *Kinkyu Torishirabe Shitsu*[1] (Emergency Interrogation Room) which was recently broadcast on TV Asahi featuring popular actress Amami Yuki whom Kishida and Namiki were particularly fond of. More excitement ensues as the women discuss the favourable changes in the portrayals of women in the popular media in Japan. More dramas have been produced in recent years featuring female characters in lead roles that realistically reflect the lives of many Japanese women today, and no longer in their traditional domestic roles as housewives as women have been depicted in the past. Yet, they also concur that these female roles are still cast in negative light. The actress Amami is said to have won numerous awards for leading roles in TV dramas since leaving the all-female Takarazuka Revue,[2] for her roles as a formidable lawyer in two seasons of *Rikon Bengoshi*[3] (Divorce Lawyer), head of a police investigation team in two seasons of *Boss*,[4] and an outstanding chef of French cuisines in *Chef: Mitsuboshi no Kyūshoku*[5] (Chef: Three Star School Lunch). In each of these dramas, the actress role is that of an intelligent, capable, independent, and strong woman, though she is also seriously flawed with 'weaknesses' typically associated with career-minded women in Japan. The strong characters that she plays are portrayed as emotional, *gōman* (arrogant), *ganko* (stubborn), *wagamama* (selfish), *han shakai teki* (anti-social), *kodoku* (solitary), and *sabishī* (lonely), as well as an *akuma* (devil), an *oni* (demon), *yōkai* (monster), and *onikuma* (bear demon).

Sawabe laughs as she mentions other TV dramas featuring another favourite actress of hers Yonekura Ryoko, who is also typecast in similar ways. The actress's image has changed radically over the years, from her lead roles as a good wife who tolerates her husband's infidelity in *Fushin no Toki*[6] (Times of Distrust), and a woman torn between career and romance in *Katagoshi no Koibito*[7] (Over-the-Shoulder Lover), to being the only female in The Special Investigation Team of police officers in *Koshonin*[8] (The Negotiator), and a short-tempered lawyer who dislikes children in *Monsuta Parento*[9] (Monster Parent). More recently, the actress plays the lead role as a freelance surgeon with extraordinary surgical skills in *Dokuta-X*[10] (Doctor-X), and as a capable, non-conformist lawyer in *Rigaru V: Gen Bengoshi*[11] (Legal V: Ex-Lawyer), though both characters are also portrayed as lonely social misfits.

Kishida and Namiki tease Sawabe for liking television programmes that overly exaggerate the strengths of women, as well as their weaknesses as anti-institution, individualistic, selfish, unpleasant, and anti-social characters. Sawabe agrees with her friends that the images are protracted, but she could at least draw some comfort from knowing that leading female roles have improved considerably from a decade ago, when TV dramas incessantly portrayed career-minded women as selfish individuals for not fulfilling their expected gender roles, and hence were typecast as nasty *oni*. Namiki chuckles as she points out to her friends that there are many TV dramas today that still portray such stereotypes of women as *oni* for being smart, independent, and capable professionals. Kishida nods and remarks:

> We have to be grateful (*winks*). It is already a big improvement. As women, we cannot ask for too much. The media in Japan would not leave us alone. We ought to feel flattered for their constant interest in women. I guess that means many people in Japan are also curious about how women have changed. Portraying women in the media is perhaps the easiest way for people to understand what we have become...
> (*laughs*)

Namiki agrees, and adds:

> That is right, Japanese women have changed so much since the war that many are confused and concerned about how we might be destroying Japanese culture (*laughs*). To portray career women well, for example, as angels, is to say that it is good for women to be strong, independent, and self-sufficient. Since it is difficult for some people to accept that, women must be with imperfections to give people comfort that women are partly to blame for some of the problems in society today...

The others laugh as they recall the numerous instances when women are blamed for a wide range of the so-called 'social problems,' from juvenile delinquency and not caring enough for the elderly, to rising divorce rates and declining birth rates. 'It is always women's fault, right?' Kishida exclaims. Turning to Takagi with a cheeky smile, she says:

> Well, you will be 40 next year. That means you will become *baba*. Congratulations, and welcome to the club! Before you realize, you will be promoted to *oni* at 50. And then, who knows, the media might start describing women beyond 60 as *akuryō* (evil spirit). The media must love us very much to give us so much attention that they turn us into powerful spirits and mysterious creatures! How could we not be proud?
> (*laughs*)

Sawabe and Namiki could not stop laughing in agreement with Kishida as they comfort Takagi, explaining that the portrayals of career women in the Japanese media have been less kind in the past. The older women have lived through years of being disparagingly referred to as *shokuba no hana* (flowers in the office), *make inu* (loser dogs), *sararī gāru* (salaried girls), *parasaito shinguru* (parasite singles), and many more derogatory labels that proliferated in Japan over the past decades. The real problem, Kishida says, is that many people in Japan would not accept that many women could not perform their expected gender roles in Japanese society while they are at the same time also expected to contribute to the nation's economic growth, especially during the bubble decade in the 1980s.

The popular media as a forceful barometer, creator, and promoter of social attitudes

The women's narratives highlight the dominant influence of the popular media in Japan as a forceful arena for creating, transforming, and propagating images and portrayals, as well as echoing the agendas of official policymakers, and reflecting prevailing views in Japanese society, with lasting impressions and influential impact on social attitudes and practices. The country's popular media is one of the largest, diversified, and most influential popular media industry in the world, ranging from broadcasting, film, and popular music, to newspapers, magazines, and popular literature. The information and media industries generated revenues of 531 trillion yen in 2016 (Dentsu 2018: 10), accounting for approximately 15.8 per cent of the country's total Gross Domestic Product (GDP) of 3,351 trillion yen (SHJ 2018: 24).

The broadcasting industry in Japan is alone a massive industry with a popular prime time programme gaining viewership that run into tens of millions. The industry comprises both cable and terrestrial companies; of the five largest terrestrial television networks are the public-owned *Nippon Hōsō Kyōkai* (NHK), followed by commercial broadcasters such as *Nippon Terebi Hōsōmō Kabushiki-Gaisha* (Nippon Television Network, or Nippon TV, and controlled by the Yomiuri Shimbun publishing group); *Kabushiki-Gaisha Terebi Asahi* (TV Asahi); *Kabushiki-Gaisha Terebi Tōkyō* (TV Tokyo, which is partly owned by The Nikkei, the world's biggest financial newspaper group that recently bought The Financial Times); and *Kabushiki-Gaisha Fuji Terebijon* (Fuji Television Network, or simply Fuji TV). Cable networks are privately owned, of which the largest national and regional service are Jupiter Telecommunications (J:COM), Japan Cablenet (JCN), SKY PerfecTV!, WOWOW, and Hikari TV. All the aforementioned companies also provide satellite broadcast domestically and overseas.

The popular literature business is also a huge industry which comprises more than 3,434 companies in 2016 (Ibid.: 4), publishing books, magazines, *manga* (comics), and other print media, through multiple channels, including direct sales, online, bookstores, and at convenience stores. Sales volume of the print media industry totalled 1.98 trillion copies, with revenues of 1.47 trillion yen, while the *manga* industry alone had reported sales of 669 million copies in 2016 generating revenues of 195 billion yen (Ibid.).

More importantly, each of the country's two largest advertising and marketing companies Dentsu Inc. and Hakuhodo Inc., which rank among the largest in the world, operates a highly integrated networks of advertising and marketing – which span from the print media and broadcast operations, to digital networks and event management – and dominates nearly the entire domestic market. Media discourses and trends thus proliferate rapidly, simultaneously, consistently, and persistently in Japan to exert considerable power in introducing, changing, and reinforcing attitudes, beliefs, perceptions, and everyday practices. As such, they often have far-reaching ramifications on individuals and social relations.

The popular media have played a critical role in disseminating images and discourses on Japanese women in particularly forceful ways, at times echoing bureaucratic voices of conservatism, and at other times those of the more progressive and liberal. A vast amount of discourses on and images of Japanese women, especially those who are working and have professional careers, have proliferated over the past few decades to exert considerable pressure and instil immeasurable anxiety on these segments of the population in the country that many women have come to experience confused identities and conflicted desires, amidst growing opportunities for them to pursue alternative lifestyles beyond the realm of domesticity. As the women's aforementioned narratives suggest, shifting media discourses have, since the economic bubble era in the 1980s, both reflected prevailing social attitudes towards working women and imposed considerable influence on women's own experiences of conflict, frustrations, and discontent in managing their lives in relation to the wide-ranging media portrayals and discourses.

Among the most persistent are those of women's rightful place in Japanese society in the home, and their expected roles as mothers, wives, and care-givers, despite the unrelenting and consistent demands of the state and corporations for women as a pool of 'cheap,' 'under-utilized,' and 'expendable resource' (Waswo 1996: 154), in response to the vagaries of growth and recession of the broader economy. The notion of the *hataraku josei* (working women) is not only a contradiction, but it is also 'confusion of categories' (Creighton 1996: 215). Men's work is seen as the main economic source for the family, while women's work is to support their husband and supplement the household income. Women with professional careers are more problematic, as their career pursuits pose a threat to men's ability to provide for the family. The corporate workplace has, is, and will continue to be a gendered environment symbolic of masculine identity (Goodman 2002: 41), and where women as 'professional women' are regarded as 'mavericks...who for one reason or another failed to find a husband, or those who were later widowed or divorced sought careers in employment' (Waswo 1996: 148). This perhaps explains why many female corporate workers have historically been hired to perform marginal tasks and play supporting roles as *OLs* (office ladies), working in clerical, secretarial, and administrative positions (Ogasawara 1998), and taking up pink-collar jobs fit for women, as teachers (albeit below the tertiary level), nurses, care workers, cleaners, and cooks (though not as professional chefs).

Despite the phenomenal increase in the number of female corporate workers in Japan, they are not widely regarded in the same way as *shakaijin*[12] (social person) that Japanese men are, as *sararīman*. Interestingly, though expectedly, the terms *sararī boi* (salaried boy) and *bijinesu boi* (business boy) have never been used to describe young male workers, while *sararī gāru* and *bijinesu gāru* (business girl) are often fairly common. The use of gender qualifier for women suggests that *sararī gāru*, *bijinesu gāru*, and *sararī ūman* do not command the same respect and regard as that of *sararīman*, which remains to this today as symbolic of the exemplary Japanese worker. The proliferation of media discourses on and portrayals of female corporate workers reflect more than the prevailing perceptions of women in Japanese society, but also the difficulty and struggle among many to accept to come to terms with and to recognize women as individuals seeking economic independence and pursuing careers for self-fulfilment, rather than for the family. For Japan's growing female workforce, staying employed in a corporate environment is hence also a constant struggle with conflicted identities, confused senses of the self, and frustrated purpose.

The most challenging, and also conflicting, moments in Japan's post-war history occurred perhaps during the bubble decade in the 1980s, when the country's booming financial services and retail sectors introduced management-track careers to women in unprecedented numbers, with the purpose of training female employees to serve a growing female customer base (Lam 1993: 198). It was during the same period that the Japanese government was promoting the dream of Japan as a *chūryū shakai* (middle-class society), the *sararīman* (salaried man or white-collar male worker) as the male ideal, and *sengyō shufu* (professional housewife or full-time housewife) as the female ideal. Intense contradictions and debates emerged as more women entered the corporate workplace; both marriage rates and fertility rates in the country went on a descent; and Japan's miraculous economic growth began to stall. Popular media discourses and images closely traced the series of change and contradictions, as the following narratives of several other women managers will demonstrate.

From *parasaito shinguru* to *onibaba*

Many women managers who are in their forties and fifties today are still able to vividly recall what it was like to work during the bubble decade in 1980s, and also after the demise of bubble economy from the early 1990s. Few could forget their experiences of having to manage their desired and real identity vis-à-vis media representations of working women over the past few decades. In reality, many of these media discourses still persist even today, though new ones have emerged in recent years to expand the spectrum of representations and discourses, and also reflect the current social attitudes towards women with professional careers. An unusual gathering of six women managers (excluding the ethnographer) several years ago captured the ethos and sentiments rather aptly. I had known these corporate executives since the early 2000s while I was posted to work in Tokyo as a corporate manager myself, and had engaged discussions with them on numerous occasions. One summer gathering was particularly enlightening, as these corporate workers elaborated in detail on how they had to manage their working lives since the bubble decade in relation to discourses in the popular media and portrayals of women with professional career in Japan.

Memoto Mio decided to organize an evening out with five of her friends while I was in Tokyo on a warm July evening. These former colleagues are busy finance executives, and the topics of their conversations at the *izakaya* (Japanese-styled bar and restaurant) in Shinagawa that Friday are, as always, dominated by discussions on statutory reporting, account consolidations, financial planning, budget forecasting, corporate restructuring, and changes to tax laws and audit regulations. After the first round of beer and light starters, the 49-year-old Memoto, who works as Financial Controller in a mid-sized European company, shares with her friends an amusing incident in her office earlier in the week, and asks if they would consider renaming their little group of colleagues-turned-friends as *onibaba kai*[13] (group of demonic old hags). Since they are all aged above 40 years, they are now able to live up to the prevailing media discourse on middle-aged women – especially women with professional career whom many regarded as bossy, domineering, and difficult – as *onibaba*. She reminds them of a suggestion made by Hirai Hanako many years back when they were co-workers that they named their little circle as *PS-kurabu* (P.S. club). The popular media had at that time popularized the term *parasaito shinguru* (literally, parasite single) coined by sociologist Yamada Masahiro (1999) in his book *Parasaito Shinguru no Jidai*[14] (The Age of the Parasite Single). Hirai, the 52-year-old Senior Finance Manager, remembers that she had said then that all of them were single, several were living with their parents, and their lifestyles fitted the descriptions of *parasaito shinguru* as self-indulgent working women who preferred consuming for their own pleasure to performing duties as wives and mothers (Kingston 2004: 273–4).

They laugh at how they still fit the descriptions today, even after nearly two decades have lapsed. 'Yes, we are all still *parasite singles* in so many different ways,' Memoto exclaims with a proud look on her face. She and Soma Seiko are not married, while Iwaki Ikue has divorced with no child, and Fukuda Fumiko is a divorced single mother of one. They are all *shinguru baba* (middle-aged, single women). While Hirai is married, she has no child, and hence fits the sociologist's descriptions of *parasaito shinguru* being a selfish and irresponsible woman who refuses to perform her dutiful role in society as mother. Iwaki corrects her friend and cites recent discussions on some television chat shows as referring to 'single' as 'someone eligible for marriage.' Three of them are simply too old to be regarded as desirable marriage partners by most Japanese men. Memoto could not stop chuckling as she teases her friend:

> Oh no, if that is the case, then none of us qualifies as *parasaito shinguru*! Shall we create a new word…hmmm how does *parasaito baba* (parasite middle-aged women) sound? Would *parasaito onibaba* (parasite demonic old hags) be better? Is it too long to pronounce?

Her remark sends the women laughing so loud that an *izakaya* attendant soon comes running to our table to convey a customer's request for us to lower our volume.

As the jollity subsides, Soma wonders if she is wrong to assume that *onibaba* came from an old Japanese folk tale about a strange, lonely old woman who seduced and killed boys and young men late at night. The 48-year-old Treasury Manager's question sparks a long discussion on how the term has recently re-emerged in the popular media after the publication of *Onibabaka suru Onnatachi* (The Trend of Women Becoming Demonic Hags) by Misago Chizuru (2004), a reproductive health specialist. Advocating marriage and childbirth, the author offers advice in her book to unmarried and childless women to not deprive themselves of the joy of childbirth and the pleasure of regular marital sex, without which women would risk damaging their mental and physical well-being, and face the danger of turning into she-ogres or demonic hags. The book became an instant bestseller, selling more than 200,000 copies within the first two years of its launch (Yamaguchi 2006: 113), and has triggered a lot of media interest and widespread online discussions.

The women scream in disbelief that an educated woman such as the author would hold such conservative views that no good could come from over-educating women or from following western ideas about feminism. Iwaki suddenly remembers having watched an old horror movie *Onibaba*[15] which her mother would often use to warn Iwaki and her younger sister against not marrying. 'My mother still talks about the book, and believes that all unmarried women will turn into demons,' the 46-year-old Human Resource Senior Manager chuckles. The other women too begin exchanging stories about their own mother's remarks about how unmarried, post-menopausal women become *onibaba* in order to release their sexual frustrations and reproductive desires by sexually assaulting younger men. In short, they all agree that women who do not perform their expected domestic roles in Japan are perceived as nasty, mean, manipulative, and a serious threat to society.

'What about unmarried Japanese men?' Hirai wonders. 'They too also become weird and threatening, and some even rape women out of frustrations and anger, no?' Memoto responds with a laugh, 'Perhaps they should be called *onijiji* (demonic old men)!' Why has such a label not appeared anywhere in the Japanese media, and why is *oni* (demonic) always associated with women but not with *jiji* (old men), Iwaki questions further. The women continue to discuss why Japanese men who behave badly would at worse be described as *kusojiji* (nasty old men) or *rōgandō* (impish old men), but that these are not as derogatory as the reference to middle-aged and older women as *kusobaba* (nasty women). Memoto sighs as she laments that not only are unmarried women being constantly scrutinized and criticized, but that married women too are not spared by the popular media.

Fukuda then turns to the ethnographer and starts teasing me. Does anyone here know that the recent popularity of media discourses on *onibaba* has piqued this researcher's interest so much that she has decided to buy the entire series of several television dramas on DVD, and has watched all of them several times? The others laugh as the 43-year-old Logistics and Billing Manager lists each title of my latest collection. This includes two seasons of *Oniyome Nikki*[16] (Diary of a Demonic Daughter-in-Law), which has been adapted from an Internet blog[17] written by a male persona as a journal on the various ways in which his wife abuses him on a daily basis. The drama portrays the shrewd and thrifty young wife who managed the finances of the family's public bath business by restricting the expenditure of her husband and father-in-law. She spends lavishly on herself instead by learning flamenco dance, which she justifies as necessary for alleviating the stress of managing the family business, and for looking after a very young daughter. In each episode, the man would devise a trick or excuse to go out with his father and male friends to drink and gamble, but he would always be caught and punished by his wife. Frustrated and sad, the man later finds comfort in an Internet blog, where he freely expresses his feelings to an anonymous community of people. The popularity of the first series *Oniyome Nikki* later spawned a wide range of popular literature and *manga* (Japanese comics), including *Tomizu Ken's Diary About His Wife* (2008), *True Accounts of the Demonic Daughter-in-*Law (2005), and two volumes of comics entitled *True Accounts of the Demonic Daughter-in-Law* (2006).

Only two women have watched parts of the drama, while the others have heard about it from their co-workers and magazines. Most of them agree that the programme is rather boring, likening it to the self-help guide *Josei no Hinkaku* (Qualities of a Woman), which is placed prominently in many bookstores for several years to taunt women to regain their lost feminine charm. 'Has anyone read it?' The women ask one another. In the book, the author Bando Mariko (2006) reminds Japanese women to not be too set in their ways of thinking or doing things, but to constantly groom themselves into becoming well-mannered, sophisticated, assertive, and feminine. While Bando's book seems to address all women, it specifically urges women above 40 years of age – both housewives and those who are working – to realize the importance of fun, enjoyment, and love in marriage or a love relationship with a man. Only the observance of this 'golden rule' would prevent women from becoming decrepit *onibaba* (Ibid.: 212).

As Memoto's explanations of the book spark another round of laughter, she jokingly urges the others to get used to being called *onibaba*. Soma responds by saying that *onibaba* conjures up the image of a *majo* (witch), which might not be a bad one after all, since American television is swamped with programmes about witches, vampires, and women with supernatural powers. Iwaki adds that the repetitive utterance of the word *onibaba* makes her feel elevated in status to resemble the formidable and intimidating Empress Dowager Cixi[18] (*seitaigo*) who ruled China in the nineteenth century. Hirai looks confounded, and laughs as she remarks:

> From *parasaito shinguru* to *onibaba*, it is amazing that we have been given so many names and yet none fits our true image. But these are just

a few that we have been given since we started working, right? My, the media have really been watching over us and tracking our growth all these years!

Women as *flowers* and *office ladies* in the corporate workplace

The women soon begin reminiscing about their early days when they started working in the 1980s and 1990s, reflecting on how different their lives are from those of their mothers, and also many of their peers whose lives are confined to domesticity. 'We are really lucky to have been born after the war, are we not?' says Hirai. 'We could work because we all attended university, unlike many of our mothers.' Memoto nods, as she remembers the excitement over dinner when her father opened a letter and informed the family that his eldest daughter had been accepted by a prestigious university in Tokyo. It was the 1980s, when Japan's economy was growing at a rapid pace and white-collar jobs for women were in abundance. Memoto's younger sister was too eager to start working that she decided to not proceed to university after completing high school. Memoto's decision to attend university was, therefore, a relief for her father, who had long cherished the hope of having at least one daughter be a university graduate. The elderly man later advised Memoto that the easiest way for a woman to secure a good job and be promoted quickly in Japan was to pursue a career in fields which women were thought to excel in, such as finance, marketing, public relations, corporate communications, and human resources. Memoto laughs as she recounts her father's advice to her to not be so ambitious as to pursue a career in law or medicine, since opportunities were extremely limited for women. Memoto's father, who had worked in the sales division of a large Japanese chemicals company, also warned his daughter to not aim too high. The ceiling for women was not made of glass, but of thin, wooden planks which would break easily and cause serious injury. The women roar so loudly on hearing the old man's words that Soma spills wine on her shirt and dashes off to the lavatory to remove the stain.

Soma returns to find Iwaki in the midst of her own father's concerns and advice before the latter left her hometown in Kyoto to work in the capital. You should work for a few years to find a good husband, and then get married, give birth, and be the proud wife of a successful *sararīman* and the proud mother of highly educated children, she imitates his tone of voice. A woman's education must be put to such good purposes and not be wasted on individual pursuits, he had said. A woman is ultimately *shokuba no hana*, which will wither quickly and be replaced, and so she must herself set a desirable marriage target of a successful or potentially successful man while she is in bloom. Iwaki's adeptly re-enactment of her father's stern countenance as he uttered those words triggers yet another round of uncontrollable laughter. After the banging of the dinner table and wiping of tears have subsided, the five friends continue to discuss how the elderly men's views were not only prevalent back in the 1980s, but that they are also common even today. Female university graduates like themselves who become white-collar workers are often regarded as flowers in the workplace. Many are also regarded as *sararī gāru* and *bijinesu gāru*. In short, they are mere *gāru* (girls) with no serious intention of pursuing any long-term, professional career, and so they are not to be taken seriously (see Iwao 1993: 156). The thought that their own fathers had such little hope for them to become professionals in their respective career pursuits made the women sigh and lament their misfortune of being born female.

'But it was *baburu no jidai* (the bubble era), and any woman with a decent education could get a fairly good job and lead an economically independent life,' Hirai recalls, and all her friends agree. Still, Fukuda retorts, the idea of women doing *ippan shoku* (ordinary work, as in having a full-time job in an office) was relatively new during the 1980s. Many people in Japan were not accustomed to the idea of women pursuing a professional career. Women working in offices were said to be doing *jimu shoku* (clerical work) which were not different from various other non-office jobs performed by women, such as cleaning, cooking and babysitting, hairdressing, nursing, and teaching. Also known as 'pink-collar jobs' (Lebra 1984: 227), these types of work were deemed suitable for women to perform their socially expected gender roles as *tsuma* (wives) and *haha oya* (mothers), and were hence conferred a lower status than jobs intended for Japanese men (Iwao 1993: 156). Even after marriage, women were perceived to be useful to work in a family business or an 'appropriately feminine job' and not to perform any other 'unnecessary and unwise' tasks (Waswo 1996: 148). The five friends continue to discuss how women's jobs were in the past often described in domestic terms, and are still talked about in this manner today. Marriage, for example, is called a woman's *eikyū shūshoku* (lifetime employment). While many Japanese women had in the past tended to work in *kagyō* (family businesses) of their natal family or of their husband's, many married women also took work within the neighbourhoods where they lived doing various jobs pertaining to sewing, babysitting, and cleaning that are called *naishoku* (private jobs) because they were similar to their own household chores (Iwao 1993: 156). For educated women, their jobs in offices were often described as *koshikake* (a chair, a temporary seat, or momentary job), which was intended for giving women *shakai kengaku* (an experience of the world outside the home) (Ibid.). Many women would quit their jobs after getting married or to give birth, though a large number of them would return to the workforce after childbirth to supplement their household incomes, or to support themselves following a divorce. This pattern is still prevalent in Japan today, though many female workers who return to the labour force are hired as *pāto* (part-time workers) in department stores and factories. The temporary or part-time work that they do is at times also referred to as *arubaito* (which was borrowed from the German verb for work *arbeiten*), or abbreviated further as *baito*.[19]

Unlike many women in pre-war Japan who were confined to the home as housewives, Memoto and her friends view themselves as *shakai ni detteta onna* (women who went out into society). Also, unlike many Japanese women who worked in the 1950s and 1960s, the five friends belong to the first generation of Japanese women to be given unprecedented opportunities to pursue management-track careers in large corporations. Contrary to many of their parents' expectations and wishes, all of my informants have remained in full-time employment for many years after graduating from high school or university. Some of their parents had expressed concerns about the risks these women faced as *kyaria ūman* (career women). Iwaki recalls how her parents had panicked over her turning into a *kurisumasu kēki*[20] (Christmas cake) when she was still unmarried at 29 years of age, and decided to intensify the search for a potential son-in-law by arranging *omiai* (matchmaking) for her every week. The search stopped after several months, due partly to the exorbitant costs involved, and because of their growing embarrassment over their daughter's lack of popularity. Her father was particularly opposed to Iwaki's intention of pursuing a professional career in finance. When she mentioned her plans to study for the American Certified Professional Accountant (CPA) qualification, he warned her of the 'risk' of being a spinster for the rest of her life. No Japanese man would want to marry a woman who is more professionally qualified than he is, or who has a more successful career than his, Iwaki's father had said. But she was more disappointed by her mother's comments that Iwaki could study for the qualification as a leisure activity after marriage and childbirth, and so that she must first find a good husband whose job and income are good enough to support the family and her hobbies.

How views and attitudes are yet to change much even today, the women lament. Then, Memoto tries to lighten the mood of the evening by making her friends laugh again at her own father's anxiety over the endless after-work drinking and entertaining activities that she had to participate in. She recalls a discussion one evening with the old man who said that women could not climb the corporate ladder in the same way as men could. His reason was that the late-night world of drinking and entertainment in Japan was catered to the pleasures of men, and it was improper for women to do the same. Memoto's mother then interrupted her father, and demanded for details of the activities that he and his co-workers had often engaged in that were improper for women. A little family drama soon followed, as her father continued to evade the question while her mother insisted on having a response. The old man was ordered by his wife to sleep on the couch for weeks, but was permitted to sleep in the couple's bedroom after he made considerable effort to return home early from work to have dinner with his wife regularly. 'What a fun family,' Soma exclaims with a chuckle.

Memoto later elaborates on several conversations that she and her sister had with their father – in his wife's absence, obviously – about his late-night voyeuristic activities at hostess clubs and other places. He could not stop worrying about his young daughters' late-night drinking with co-workers. I have also learned about some of his past encounters when I was staying with the family. Business is *otoko no shakai* (men's world), where women's roles are in the *mizushōbai* (water business, which refers to venues for drinking, voyeuristic play, and even paid sex), as *shōbai onna* (women in the water business), says Memoto as she mimicks her father's facial expression and tone of voice, which triggered another round of laughter. While the old man was later comforted to know that his daughters had become good drinkers who could share many rounds of beer and other alcoholic beverages with him after his retirement, he could at times express regrets that they were not born as sons instead. The women laugh again, and exchange more stories on their own parents' concerns about their having to drink in *sakariba* (district populated with places for late-night drinking and entertainment). Yet, their parents' fears were not unfounded. Several women did have awkward encounters. Iwaki and Fukuda, for example, have had to join their co-workers and superiors to a hostess club and a strip show. Memoto and Hirai have also been pressured, but refused to do so. They have been, however, refused entry to a bar on a few occasions and were told that the venues were for 'gentlemen only.'

Memoto laughs at how most Japanese men are unwilling to acknowledge the fact that many women in Japan do drink and play – including paying for sex and having extramarital experiences – as much as their male counterparts. She is glad, though, that many late-night entertainment venues have become available to women after the bubble decade. Indeed, there has been a radical change to the urban night-time economy in post-bubble Japan. The phenomenal increase in the number of white-collar female workers has prompted the commercial sector – especially operators of love hotel, host clubs, strip bars, and various other entertainment establishments, as well as producers of alcoholic beverages – to target this growing yet untapped market (Chaplin 2007; Ho 2008, 2012a, 2015; Marx 25 March 2010; Suzuki 2002).

Does this mean that *hataraku dansei* (working men) could also mean male prostitutes and hosts? Soma giggles as she poses another question to her friends. Since when did *hataraku josei* (working women) or *wākingu ūman* (working woman) become associated with prostitution like the label *shōbai onna*? Hirai wonders too, and asks how *hataraku josei*, which is widely used in the media, including by the respectable Nikkei Woman,[21] could have such shady associations? Memoto laughs as she takes an electronic dictionary out of her bag and searches for the word *shokugyō fujin* (woman with a vocation or occupation). Well, the Japanese Kojien Dictionary explains this as 'women who have gone out into society from the home and engaged in working activities during those times when very few women actually did so.'[22] However, the dictionary makes no reference to prostitution or prostitutes. Puzzled and curious, the conversation turns to discussing the limited job options Japanese women had in the past other than to work in a family business, such as a farm, shop, or factory. Those who had received payment for their labour elsewhere were mostly *shōbai onna* – as hostesses, entertainers, and prostitutes – since the *mizushōbai* (such as hostess clubs, strip bars, and massage parlours) was the main – or only – industry that would hire women in large numbers (Allison 1994: 7; Inoue 1999: 8; Seigle 1991: 8; Suzuki 2002: 108). Fukuda wonders if the term *bijinesu ūman* is merely the modern version of *shōbai onna*, as she has heard that many women working in *mizushōbai* describe themselves as *bijinesu ūman*. Her friends agree in unison, and discuss how many Japanese companies and businesses have in the past decades grown to prefer the English word *bijinesu* to the old-fashioned Japanese references *shōbai* and *kigyō* to project a modern image of themselves.

Conflicted independence as 'children of the bubble'

The bubble era did bring a lot of changes in Japan, especially for the women managers. Many large Japanese corporations were relatively indifferent to women's career development issues until the mid-1970s, when an expansion of the service sector demanded a significant transformation of the employment structure that led to an increase in the demand for more female labour (Lam 1993: 198). Between 1975 and 1985, the total employed labour force expanded by 18 per cent. While male employment rose by 12 per cent, female employment jumped by 33 per cent (Ibid.). Many retail companies in Japan were among the first to organize female employees into small groups to improve productivity and customer services, which led many employers to create supervisory positions for their female employees. This was followed by the banking and insurance industries in the 1980s, when companies began promoting female leadership with the aim of training future female workers (Ibid.: 198–201). Each of these women managers began her first job in one of these industries.

For Memoto, the few months after her graduation from university with a degree in Finance were spent not on job-hunting, but choosing a job among the numerous offers that she had received. They were all from companies in the retail and service industries, though. Even after she had decided to join the finance department of a large American consumer toy producer where she worked for three years, she was constantly invited by business acquaintances to move to their respective companies. Unable to resist the tempting offers, she moved to another American retail conglomerate where she worked her way from the position of Sales Supervisor to Branch Manager of a new store, and enjoyed numerous overseas trips for training and business for five years. As *baburu no kodomotachi* (children of the bubble), the women did not lack the opportunity to advance their careers or develop an economically independent lifestyle. As Memoto recalls:

> We are fortunate to be *baburu no kodomotachi*, right? I was so impatient to graduate from university because I could not control my excitement… to have a job, an income, my own apartment, and a lifestyle that would be so different from my mother's.

> Our careers were made by the bubble, for the bubble, and during the bubble...it was a time of choice, freedom and independence. Jobs were available anytime and anywhere that we did not need a degree from the University of Tokyo to get a good job with a good salary, unless we wanted to work for the government. I somehow knew that this would not last but while it did we could do everything that women in the past could only dream about...

Memoto's comments point to the expansion of Japan's services, finance, banking, and retail sectors, which had played a particularly important role in driving the increase in the number of clerical, professional, and managerial positions for women. There was an increase in the employment of women – most of whom were university graduates – in white-collar jobs and knowledge-intensive occupations from 11 per cent in 1955, to 24 per cent in 1970, and to 35 per cent in 1980 (Mizuno 1984: 24). However, some social commentators were sceptical about these opportunities. As Alice Lam (1993: 198–201) notes, while the number of female employees increased by 3.8 million between 1975 and 1985, approximately 40 per cent of female employees in 1985 worked in the service industries, and 30 per cent were in the wholesale and retail industries. Moreover, these industries were 'traditionally female-intensive sectors,' and the women's jobs as 'feminine types of work' (Ibid.: 198), which were lower in status than the types of work that Japanese men did. Lam further argues that the reason for the increased demand for women employees by Japan's consumer market was driven by the general perception that Japanese women had a greater control of the family budget and were the main consumers for the family. Since women were the main target customers whose needs were thought to be better understood by women rather than by men, the development and marketing of products for women, therefore, required 'women's ideas.' Given also that women were regarded as better at managing female employees, many large Japanese corporations turned to promoting women to supervisory and managerial positions for the sole purpose of training and managing junior female workers.

The women managers were aware of such 'traditional' ideas held by employers during the 1980s. They remembered having been told by employers to treat the *kaisha* (company) as their *ie* (home), where it was necessary for men and women to do different jobs in order to raise efficiency and productivity of their employer's business. As *kazoku* (family), employees were like siblings of different ages and hierarchical positions who must perform tasks assigned to them without trying to compete for another employee's job or to replace another. If a woman was to compete to do a man's job, she would disrupt other people's work and even render the work of others ineffective. The women laughed at the reference to that of the *ie* (household system) that was propagated during the Meiji period following the collapse of the Tokugawa Shogunate from the late 1860s. The women remembered being told to read several publications by popular Japanese intellectuals at that time to motivate employees to be proud of being *nihonjin* (Japanese) and to accept the seemingly unjust corporate system as an important and necessary way for Japan to gain greater economic success. Soma and Memoto remember having to read books which explained Japan as a hierarchically structured and naturally group-oriented but harmonious society. Hirai and Iwaki too have had to do readings while in university which praised Japanese society's group-oriented system of work as efficient and productive, since such a system fostered mentorship as a mother provided care for her infants. Fukuda heaves a big sigh of relief for not being forced to read any of these works, and remarks cynically that the state and companies always work in collusion to persuade workers like themselves who were so willing and eager to derive gains during those bubble years of economic prosperity.

These works mentioned earlier were published by many Japanese scholars between the late 1970s and the late 1980s which were promoted by the state as influential texts during the bubble decade to promote theories known as *nihonjinron* about the uniqueness of the Japanese people and Japanese culture that had miraculously transformed Japan into the world's second largest economy at that time (Ho 2018: 28–9). These works – especially those by Nakane Chie and Doi Takeo – also served to reinforce the patriarchal, hierarchical, and maternal aspects of Japanese society.[23] Many others were to build on arguments made by Nakane and Doi to explain Japan's hierarchically structured society as unequal, but harmonious system that binds a mother and her children in equilibrium, hence justifying the importance of preserving Japan as a *bosei shakai*[24] (maternal society). In doing so, many of these *nihonjinron* discourses were to successfully revive the Meiji notion of the *ie* (Goodman 2005; Yoda 2006: 247), and also reinforce the Meiji promulgation of the Confucian feminine ideals of *ryōsai kenbo*[25] (Good Wives Wise Mothers) to justify the sexual division of labour in Japanese society during the period of rapid economic expansion (Uno 1993; White 2002: 126).

Fukuda is amused by the reference to Japan as a *bosei shakai* that she has heard frequently, arguing that every aspect of life in Japan actually shows that the country is a *fusei shakai* (paternal society). She recalls having been made to attend company meetings organized to brief employees on how women ought to perform a given list of jobs that are suitable and ideal for women. Women are diligent, thorough, caring, patient, obedient, and good at housekeeping, and hence they should excel in departments such as office administration, human resource management, finance, corporate communications, and customer service. Her friends too have attended training workshops designed to communicate similar messages. Yet, they are amused by the irony that such conservative views have actually opened up the corporate world to women. Should they be thankful to have some opportunities than none? Ought they not be grateful to be given opportunities that were denied to women of the previous generations? There are more questions than these women managers could find a meaningful response to.

The period between the late 1970s and mid-1980s was particularly memorable and had special significance for the women under study, as the era marked their *jiritsu* (independence). With a salaried job, each of them could spend their own money and feel like *hontō na otona* (real adults). Several women had moved to Tokyo to study and later remained in the city where their management-track career enabled them to live on their own. They had to work hard, of course, but the feelings of independence and freedom were indescribable. The bubble decade was also *asobi no jidai* (an era of play). They had partied a lot when they were university students, but many had to obtain their parents' permission to stay out late at night, and were chided for returning home late. As financially independent individuals, they were free to go out almost every evening after work to shop, eat, drink, dance, sing in karaoke bars, travel domestically and overseas, and even date freely.

For these women, the bubble era marked their birth as *shakaijin*[26] (persons in society). *Shakaijin* refer to an *otona* (adult) with employment and are financially independent, and have hence achieved the status of becoming members of the broader society, with the ability to handle the complex webs of social relations that mediate their position in society (Matsunaga 2000: 54). However, *shakaijin* does not seem to apply equally to men and women. Employment is the determining factor for the former, while marriage for the latter. For Japanese men, paid work and affiliation with a company mediate their membership in Japanese society. However, full social membership for women lies in domesticity, where their rightful place involves taking up their expected roles as wives, mothers, and care-givers (Edwards 1989: 116–27). More importantly, becoming a *shakaijin* constitutes only one stage in the maturing process of gaining full maturity to attaining the status of *ichininmae* (a complete person) (Hendry 1981: 50; Lebra 1984: 78), which is again different for the two sexes. A Japanese male becomes a *shakaijin* when he has gained employment, which prepares him for becoming *ichininmae* when his economic independence enables him to take on all the responsibilities of providing for his family. The situation is the reverse for women, whose path to full personhood or *ichininmae* is achieved through marriage and motherhood (Lebra 1984: 164; Matsunaga 2000: 123). Women with full-time employment may have become *shakaijin*, but they are not considered to have attained the full status of *ichininmae* until and unless they are married and have become mothers. As discussed earlier, even if a woman is highly educated, her education is considered to groom her for marriage and motherhood instead of for pursuing a professional career (Iwao 1993: 40). Women who work are expected to quit their jobs after marriage, and especially before childbirth (Ogasawara 1998: 18; Roberts 2005: 106). As Takie Sugiyama Lebra (1984: 78) notes, 'marriage is a necessary, if not sufficient, condition for making one an adult (*ichininmae*) and a human being in the full sense of the term,' the path for women that of marriage as 'a major step toward *ichininmae*' and later of motherhood' which 'fulfils it' (Ibid.: 164). She explains further that 'to be accepted as daughter-in-law was regarded as a major step toward *ichininmae* – full adulthood – for a woman' (Ibid.: 141). For the five women and other working women in Japan, they have followed an unconventional way of attaining *ichininmae* by following that of their male counterparts. Regardless of whether these women are single, married, or divorced, many are sole breadwinners in the family, the main economic provider, or equal contributors to the household income. Yet, the view that women achieve the status *ichininmae* only through marriage and motherhood seems to have remained little changed.

Memoto and her partner have lived together since they graduated from university, preferring a more relaxed lifestyle than a typical married life. The couple shares all household expenses equally, though Memoto has been contributing more since her elderly mother moved in after her father's death. Hirai also splits all household expenditure equally with her husband, including the monthly allowance for her own parents and parents-in-law. Soma and Iwaki share with their own siblings in supporting their respective parents. Fuduka is the sole breadwinner of a family of five: her elderly mother, child, and an unemployed sibling. Given the considerable contributions these women managers make to their family's financial demands, it thus amuses them that they should not be perceived as *shakaijin* and also accorded with the status of *ichininmae*. As Memoto remarks:

> The problem is not about whether women like us are incomplete for not having a husband, a child, parents, or parents-in-law to look after. The real problem is that the Japanese government does not want to spend more money on providing adequate support for people.
>
> It is therefore the government's problem, of not wanting to change many policies and budgets on childcare, elderly care and pension. They are just conveniently passing the blame to women so that other people would say that it is women's fault, and not the government's. We are all pawns in their game of managing people's lives for the economy for their own benefits, and those of large companies.

The shift in the women's discussion on the implementation of the *Danjo Koyō Byōdōhō* or Equal Employment Opportunity Law in 1986[27] (EEOL) gives illuminating insights into understanding the state's role in perpetuating conservative views of Japanese women. Though it was implemented technically to help improve working conditions for women, the lack of proper monitoring by the state, and the absence of punitive measures imposed on companies not enforcing the new legislation rendered it effective and meaningless. The corporate executives share their experiences of having been asked to serve tea at office meetings even after the 1990s, many years after the EEOL had been implemented. Hirai makes everyone laugh when she says that she would gladly serve tea at every meeting till her retirement if her employer was willing to pay her a manager's salary. Several women instantly raise their hands and say that they too would gladly have a job like that, though Memoto waves her finger and chides her friends for being deluded into thinking that companies would pay *onibaba* to serve tea, and not young and beautiful female employees. Regardless of the law, many Japanese people – both men and women alike – would always think that it is women who serve, while men are being served. Then, pausing briefly, she adds that gender equality is an illusion and would never happen in Japan.

As studies have pointed out, the EEOL was introduced as the result of pressures from working women and activist groups in Japan who had criticized Japanese corporations for not improving on their personnel and management rules and practices despite the rapid increase in white-collar female workers in the early 1980s. Companies were said to have allocated men and women to separate career tracks, and the Japanese government had also been criticized for doing little to improve work conditions for women, especially for not providing ample childcare services for working mothers (see Fujita 1989). In a survey conducted in 1981, Japan's Ministry of Labour (which was later renamed as the Ministry of Health, Labour and Welfare or MHLW) reported that 71 per cent of companies restricted the recruitment of graduates to men only, while 83 per cent of the companies surveyed did not offer any position to women, and 43 per cent offered their female employees no promotion opportunity (MOL 1981). After the EEOL came into effect in 1986 to supposedly rectify situations such as these, the state did little to enforce equal opportunities in reality (Honda 1984: 119; Lam 1993: 208). As Alice Lam (1993: 208) remarks, the legislation interprets 'to give women equal opportunity' as 'not to exclude women and not to treat women unfavourably,' 'to exclude women' as not to offer women any opportunity, and 'not to exclude women' as to offer women some opportunity. However, the vagueness of these statements prevented many employers from being penalized for offering job promotions to more men than women so long as women were not being excluded. Lam argues further that the Ministry of Labour had not embodied the concept of 'indirect discrimination,' and was not genuinely concerned about tackling the problem of institutional discrimination (Ibid.: 208–9). Mark Rebick (2005: 114), however, remarks that the new legislation had only made it more difficult for companies to openly discriminate against women in hiring and promotion decisions, while Tanaka Michiko (1984: 5–7) contended that the law was relatively silent on the predicaments faced by working mothers (for further discussions on the legislation, see Molony 1995: 286; Ōwaki 1987: 229).

Views on the effectiveness of the EEOL remain mixed to this day. Similarly, criticisms and cynicism have also grown since the current Prime Minister Shinzo Abe announced plans in 2014 to raise the number of women managers in both the public and private sectors. The Japanese government has rolled out numerous plans which are not being monitored properly or implemented effectively that Memoto and all her friends agree that pursuing gender equality is futile. They would be better off devoting their efforts to resolving more important, practical, and pressing problems that would help them survive the impending challenges posed by the prolonged recession during the 1990s following the demise of Japan's bubble economy.

Surviving the recession as flexible, non-core corporate workers

By the early 1990s, the escalation in property prices that had fuelled Japan's miraculous economic growth in the preceding decades became unsustainable, and the economy eventually came to a grinding halt. The women remember the day when the Nikkei 225 Index had its biggest one-day crash in history in 1990[28]; the Great Hanshin Earthquake on 17 January 1995 that killed more than five thousand people; and the sarin gas attack on Tokyo's subway by a new religious group known as Aum Shinrikyō on 20 March 1995, which killed more than a dozen commuters. The ensuing years were as a period of 'depressed fathers and mothers,' as many workers were retrenched after an endless spate of corporate bankruptcies. The father of several women's friends had suffered a heart attack, become depressed, or committed suicide due to business failure, redundancy, or indebtedness. Many mothers too became depressed, hysterical, and suicidal. But for these women managers, there is no turning back to a life of domesticity even if they would like to. Having a source of income is not only necessary for their economic independence, but it is also important for protecting their self-esteem, and maintaining a strong sense of self-worth.

Yet, at the same time, it was also difficult to move forward, since jobs were in shortage during the economic recession in the early 1990s. Many women were forced to be *hakenshain* (part-time or temporary workers) for years before they could eventually secure full-time employment. Fukuda remembered a conversation with her husband:

> My husband had in the past often urged me to stop working and be a full-time housewife. He was doing well at work and said he could provide for all our expenses. But after he was demoted at work and lost all the money he had invested, he begged me to keep working. Better still, find a job that paid a high salary than his, he had said.
>
> It surprised me that he could suddenly care little about his pride or his desire to be respected as a capable sole breadwinner. All that mattered to him was that we could pay our bills and lead a reasonably stable life. Well, if a stubborn male chauvinist like him could swallow his own pride and change his views about women, so could Japanese people change their old-fashioned attitudes as well...
>
> (*laughs*)

Iwaki is doubtful, however. Her former husband has a 'huge but fragile ego' which makes him feel easily embarrassed to be perceived by others as being incapable of supporting his family as the sole breadwinner. The couple had endless fights over her 'selfishness' for being excessively focused on her own career, and refusing to be a good wife by giving birth, even though the couple could barely afford to live only on his salary as an ordinary bank employee during the recession. They eventually filed for divorce after seven years of marriage.

The women soon break into another round of laughter as they tease one another for being *make inu* (loser dogs), a metaphor to describe women who are failures in their expected gender roles as wives and mothers. They are all *make inu* or a *make gumi* (group of losers), since they are unmarried, married with no child, or divorced. 'Regardless of whether you are a *kyaria ūman* or a *sengyō shufu*, a woman could easily become a *make inu* no matter what she does!' Iwaki exclaims. Who might be *kachi inu* (winner dogs) or belong to the category of *kachi gumi*[29] (group of winners), and where did these terms come from? she wonders. I later learned that the discourse had proliferated following the publication of *Make Inu no Toboe* (Howls of the Loser Dogs) by Japanese author Soma Junko (2001), *Tōkyō Make Inu Kyōshikyoku* (The Mad Songs of Tokyo's Loser Dogs) by Makiko Yamazaki (2006), and several other authors who were all female. Beginning with criticisms against women for refusing to marry or to give birth, *make inu* later expanded in scope in the popular media to also include married women who were childless; women whose husband's incomes were too low to afford a home of their own (*mai homu*); women who could not stop their husband from having extramarital affairs; women whose children had performed poorly in school, could not obtain a good job after completing school, or became juvenile delinquents; divorced women who had failed to keep their marriage; and working mothers for neglecting their primary responsibilities as wives and mothers. Fukuda looks at each of her friends, and then makes a suggestion:

> Since all women are *make inu*, what standards are used to decide who are good *make inu* and who are bad ones. Hmmm I wonder whom among us is the worst, and who the best *make inu*…
>
> (*laughs*)

The mood brightens up as the women play at ranking one another from the best to the worst *make inu*, arguing over whether marriage or motherhood ought to be main determining factor.

Being practical and optimistic was how many white-collar female workers survived the recession. Many even thrived, though ironically due to a radical change to the structure of the job market. The bubble decade of miraculous economic growth was a time of prosperity and stability which was said to be underpinned by three core values known as s*anshu no jingi* (the three jewels) – *shushin koyō* (lifetime employment), *nenkō jōretsu* (seniority promotion), and *kigyō kumiai* (company unionism) – that characterized the Japanese employment system (Goodman 2005: 64). However, this applied only to men, and those who worked in large Japanese corporations. Few recruitment agencies existed then to help workers with change of employment.

Following the demise of the bubble economy in the early 1990s, *tenshoku* (job-changing) gradually became the dominant work norm as an increasing number of employers began replacing permanent job positions with temporary and short-term contracts.

The increasingly flexible work environment later led many Japanese men to withdraw from the job market, due to mounting frustrations and disappointments with diminishing job prospects, the inability to experience *ibasho* (sense of belonging) in a corporate workplace, and the difficulty of establishing one's social identity with a corporate entity (Brinton 2011). The 1990s was called a decade of a 'lost generation' of Japanese – male and female, adults and youths – who were on the periphery of the workforce as *furītā*[30] (freeter, or people with part-time, contingent jobs) and *nītto*[31] (NEET, which stands for 'Not in Education, Employment or Training') (Kingston 2004). This generation was said to be 'lost in transition,' since young school leavers entered the labour market only to find themselves mostly in transitory, contractual jobs that offered little in terms of job security or a stable lifestyle (Brinton 2011). For Japanese author Miura Atsushi (2005: 213), the burgeoning number of *furītā* and *nītto* pointed to the new *karyū shakai* (downward-drifting society, or low social stratum) in Japan.

Ironically, the growing labour shortage soon led to new opportunities for women to gain corporate managerial positions, albeit as *non koa* (non-core) workers, and doing *furekkusu wāku* (flexible work) or at *furekkusu taimu* (literally, 'flex time' to mean flexible work hours). Many employers continued to view women as an 'under-utilized,' 'expendable resource' to be hired and fired readily. Enterprises looking to cut operating costs once again turned to the female workforce to meet this objective. In replacing permanent positions with short-term, temporary ones, companies could hire more workers for similar levels of remuneration or less, since employers were – and still are – not required to provide irregular workers with transportation allowance, pension benefits, and various other entitlements required for full-time workers.

Still, the women had to remain employed and survive the economic recession, even if many had to endure living with the labels *furītā* and *nītto* for drifting from one job to another. Memoto and her friends had accepted jobs of short contractual durations, so much so that going for job interviews was as much a part of their daily life as their temporary employment. Several women had to change jobs every few months, while the others at least once a year. But the longer it took to search for a permanent job, the worse their resumes looked. They thus risked being perceived as incapable of staying long at a given workplace, though it was due to no fault of their own. Even after an offer for a full-time position came along and was quickly accepted, the women remember feeling constantly afraid of being made redundant again, due to restructuring or corporate cost-cutting exercise. Not only have those feelings of unsettledness, anxiety, and insecurity remained strong till today, but they have recently intensified after the government released a white paper announcing its plans to curb workplace bullying and *pawahara* (power harassment) in a new legislation to be enforced in 2020 or later. Ironically, this would give employers more novel justifications to dismiss employees deemed as 'undesirable' – for being old, expensive, or unproductive – or simply 'unlikeable' by those in position of power. Three of the five women have been dismissed on the grounds of their having harassed junior employees, an accusation which had made them feel powerless and more vulnerable than ever before. To stay competitive in the job market, in the hope of improving their chances of *kyaria kīpu* (career keep, meaning to keep their career), all five women have attended courses in the evening to acquire new professional qualifications at their own expense.

They lament that opportunities for *kyaria appu* (career up, that is, to advance one's career) have been limited, and almost non-existent, in post-bubble Japan. And the prospects were increasingly gloomier for women aged 40 years and older, who could only struggle to prevent a *kyaria daun* (career down, which means taking up job positions of lower status and salary). In reality, all five women have since the early 2010s been experiencing a decline in their career in various ways, and a sharp decrease in their income that came with a demotion or job change to a lesser position. 'What do you think?' Memoto suddenly breaks into a cheeky smile. 'Would a woman be called a *kanpeki na make inu* (perfect loser dog) for losing her career or becoming unemployed because she could neither *kyaria kīpu* nor *kyaria appu*?' Fukuda laughs as she retorts, 'No, she would turn into a *sūpā onibaba* (super demonic hag) and gain supernatural powers, since such a woman would be very old after spending years building her career, and has probably also lost her marriage, children and everything else that could make her happy and fulfilled.' Another round of laughter follows. Hirai then asks how Fukuda has managed to work for the same company for more than 12 years, when all the others have worked for more than five companies over those years. Fukuda shrugs her shoulders and explains:

> There is no secret formula. I just accept every change of position, transfer of division, and even a pay cut. What choice do I have as a non-core worker in this big company? I have to be practical and accept anything that is given to me if I want to stay employed and not be fired by the company. With so much restructuring going, my job is as insecure in this company as it would be in another. I just go with the flow, endure as much as I could, and take anything that my bosses give me, so that I could stay as long as possible... The company is always the *kachi gumi*, and we are the real *make gumi*...

As they ponder over why they are persistently being labelled by Japanese society as losers when their labour has been necessary to the broader economy, Memoto suddenly remembers that a government minister had once caused a national outrage by describing Japanese women as *kodomo no umu kikai*[32] (childbearing machines, or birth-giving machines), and for being 'selfish' in 'failing to do their best' to reproduce so as to not aggravate the country's declining birth rate or strain social welfare and pension systems further (Ito 2007). If they had been 'good' by performing their socially expected roles as wives and mothers, would their lives have been significantly different or better, Soma wonders. Hirai quickly interjects and says that women could never run away from being labelled as *make inu*, as what they do would never be good enough, regardless of whether they are *sengyō shufu* or *sararīman*. They have chosen to be *sararīman*, and survived some of the most trying years times during the prolonged recession. They must try harder to be optimistic, and hope for better times to return. Having experienced economic independence that has transformed their lifestyles, raised their expectations of a good life, and given them a strong sense of self-worth based on a professional career, these women are – to borrow Ann Waswo's (1996: 154) words – unwilling to 'retreat meekly and mutely into a purely domestic role,' and therefore have to live with the consequences of their decision.

Women managers as *sararīman* of today

A common concern among women managers in Japan that recurred during my fieldwork was what it means to be *sararīman*. Media representations of and discourses on *sararīman* are mostly about Japanese men, and rarely involve women. References to women, however, are as *sararī gāru* or *sararī ūman*. This presents significant conflicts to many women managers such as Memoto and her friends who have struggled with the problematic perceptions of women as *shakaijin* and *ichininmae*. In viewing themselves as *sararīman*, these women are not attempting to be like men. Rather, it expresses their desire to be rightly recognized as individuals who are equally capable of doing a job for a salary based on their qualifications, experience, and expertise as their male counterparts.

The *sararīman* may not have always been positively or consistently portrayed in the popular media, but it still represents an ideal of masculinity that commands a higher status than that of self-employed entrepreneurs of small, family-run businesses. The *sararīman* was once heralded as the idolized symbol of the country's 'new middle class' in the 1960s (Vogel 1971[1963]). At the pinnacle of the country's economic success in the 1980s, Japan's *sararīman* represented middle-class men who were white-collar employees of medium to large, prestigious Japanese corporations, and depicted as the 'head and provider of and for the family vis-à-vis the state' (Roberson and Suzuki 2003: 8). The *sararīman* has also been portrayed as 'a workaholic who toils long hours…goes out drinking with his fellow workers or clients after work and plays golf with them on weekends, and rarely spends much time at home with his wife and children' in the 1980s (Fujimura-Fanselow and Kameda 1995). Following the demise of the country's bubble economy, the *sararīman* was later portrayed as alcoholics (Borovoy 2005), wife batterers (Nakamura 2003), and despondents who were not to be emulated (Miura 2005). Today, the mention of *sararīman* still conjures up images of Japanese men in suits and with briefcases, drinking in groups in bars and *izakayas* across cities late at night, dozing off during their long commute home due to exhaustion or drunkenness, and even collapsing on the street in a drunken stupor. There was no lack of such representations of the *sararīman* in academic studies or the Japanese popular literature, including *anime* (animations) and *manga* (comics). Yet, however negative the associations might have become, the *sararīman* has always been, and still is, a symbol of masculinity, and not of femininity.

Many women in this study views *sararīman* as a generic term for working adults, or more specifically, corporate employees and not blue-collar workers. Still, *sararīman* remains widely regarded as a male symbol. This thus presents a conflict of identity to women with professional careers such as Memoto and her friends. The image of a typical or ideal *sararīman* in Japan is that of a white-collar male worker whose wife is a *shufu* who might hold a part-time job to supplement the family income but who manages all the household matters. It is a privilege that no female *sararīman* has ever had, nor would ever have. While there are many divorced single mothers in Japan, it is rare to find married women who are the sole family breadwinners. None of the five friends knows of any Japanese man who is willing to do what a *shufu* does, that is, be a stay-at-home husband or father who lives on his wife's income alone. Indeed, the epithet 'Good Husbands Wise Fathers' has never been incorporated as part of the male ideal in Japan as *ryōsai kenbo* has for women. Many women managers use the male reference *sararīman* to describe themselves partly to differentiate themselves from housewives, and also to avoid the flotilla of derogatory labels and images that the women have had to live with, especially when none comes close to realistically portraying their lives as women with professional careers.

The women's experience of conflicted identity has been made more difficult following the country's educational reforms in the late 1980s which began promoting ideas about 'individuality,' and groomed a new generation of Japanese to embrace the importance of *jikohakken* (self-discovery), *jibunrashī seikatsu* (lifestyle of one's choice), *jūjitsukan* (self-fulfilment), and a wide range of other discourses on the self (Ho 2018: 31). These reforms were ideologically driven by the office of former Prime Minister Nakasone Yasuhiro to propel economic growth by producing the future generation of self-motivated and 'ready' workers to help companies reduce staff training costs (Cave 2001: 177; Mouer and Sugimoto 1986: 196). However, continued promulgations of a wide range of neoliberal discourses on freedom, choice, individuality, dream, and passion by both the state and the commercial sector have transformed the aspirations and self-perceptions of many in Japan (Miyoshi and Harootunian 1989; Sakai 1989; Yoda 2006: 41). To many women managers aged below 40 years whom I have interviewed, to be *sengyō shufu* is only an option and no longer a necessity, but to be *sararīman* is necessary and the main choice in life. Many are acutely aware of their place in the male-dominated corporate world as that of *non koa* workers labouring for the broader economy under the new slogan of womenomics. While many may also feel more vulnerable being at the bottom of the corporate structure, they are less willing to tolerate injustices and unfair treatment in the workplace, and would readily voice their concerns publicly, and especially in the social media. But these could, at times, lead to identity conflicts with serious consequences on the emotional and mental health of young women managers who may be highly educated, but are relatively not as adaptable, experienced, or willing to compromise and strategize as those who are older.

The aforementioned narratives elucidate the pervasive influence of discourses in the popular media and popular literature in Japan on the everyday lives of many women pursuing a professional career in Japan. They also indicate also that popular images and representations often filter into the broader society through repeated discussions to become benchmarks for individuals to evaluate themselves and others against desired or undesirable ideals, and could, therefore, become important barometers of sociocultural values and attitudes. Despite the phenomenal increase in the number of white-collar female workers over the past few decades, attitudes towards female corporate employees, and particularly towards those who have climbed the corporate ladder to managerial positions, have not only remained conservative, but at times changed for the worse. The persistent treatment of women as a cheap labour workforce to meet the varying needs of the economy is perhaps the main factor in reinforcing the 'confusion' of the categories of women and salaried work. The implications could at times lead to unpleasant and difficult experiences, which could be particularly unbearable in the workplace. In the following chapter, a closer scrutiny will be made on how some women managers struggle with and strategize ways to cope with prevailing portrayals of and attitudes towards them in their daily interactions with co-workers through their after-work drinking activities.

Notes

1 The primetime TV drama series *Kinkyu Torishirabe Shitsu*– written by Inoue Yumiko, and directed by Tsunehiro Jota and Motohashi Keita – was first broadcast on TV Asahi Corporation (hereafter, TV Asahi) in 2014, followed by the second season in 2017. Actress Amami Yuki plays the role of Makabe Yukiko, the only female detective in the five-member *Kintori* team which works closely with two other male detectives in the Tokyo Metropolitan Police Department to interrogate suspects in accordance to a new law in Japan enacted to require all police interrogations be recorded in order to minimize police brutality.

2 *Takarazuka Kagekidan* is an all-female musical theater troupe based in the Hyōgo Prefecture near Osaka founded in 1913 by Ichizo Kobayashi, an industrialist-turned-politician and president of Hankyu Railways. The Broadway-styled productions cover Western-styled musicals, and stories adapted from *manga* and Japanese folktales. Amami Yuki played the lead male parts known as *otokoyaku* from 1987 till 1995.

3 *Rikon Bengoshi* was first broadcast on primetime television by Fuji Television Network (hereafter, Fuji TV) in 2004, followed by a second season in 2005. The series is about varied cases relating to divorce handled by Takako Mamiya, who passed the difficult Japan's bar exam on her first attempt after graduating from the country's most prestigious Tokyo University, and set up her own private practice after working for a prominent law firm.
4 *Boss* written by Hirai Koji, and directed by Mitsuno Michio and Hoshino Kazunari. It ran for two seasons on primetime television broadcast by Fuji TV in 2009 and 2011. Amami played the role of Osawa Eriko, chief of a new Special Crimes Unit formed in response to public dissatisfaction with new kinds of crime and dropping arrest rates. Though professionally competent, Osawa was featured as a single, career-obsessed character who would turn to life-sized manukins.
5 The ten-episode TV drama *Mitsuboshi no Kyūshoku*, written by Hamada Hideya, and directed by Hirano Shin and Tanaka Ryo, was broadcast on primetime television by Fuji TV in 2016. Amami played the role of Hoshino Mitsuko, a professionally trained chef of French cuisines whose determination to pursue her career led her former husband to end their marriage and take custody of their only daughter.
6 *Fushin no Toki* was broadcast by Fuji TV in 2006.
7 *Katagoshi no Koibito* was shown on Tokyo Broadcasting System (hereafter, TBS) in 2007.
8 *Koshonin* was first broadcast by TV Asahi in 2008.
9 *Monsuta Parento* was broadcast by Fuji TV in 2008.
10 *Dokuta-X* was broadcast by TV Asahi over five seasons, from 2012 till 2017.
11 *Rigaru V: Gen Bengoshi* was broadcast by TV Asahi in 2018.
12 The term *shakai* means 'society' or 'social,' and *jin* means person. When combined, the word *shakaijin* refers to a 'person in society,' as someone who has entered the job market and gained financial independence (Matsunaga 2000: 54).
13 Literally, the word *oni* means 'demonic,' while *baba* is a derogatory term for 'old hag.'
14 Yamada defines a 'parasite single' as 'an unmarried child who lives with his/her parents even after graduation and is dependent on them for his/her basic living conditions.' After the term was made popular in the Japanese media, it also sparked a series of public debates about the growing trend in unmarried Japanese (for more discussions on the topic, see Sarada 1998; Shirai 2005; Wada 2004).
15 Produced by Japanese director Shindō Kaneto in 1964, the horror movie *Onibaba* is about two women during the Nanboku period (1336–1392) who killed samurais and sold their weapons for a living. This reference was made popular again in 2005 by a television series *Oniyome Nikki* (A Demonic Daughter-in-law's Diary) broadcast by Fuji TV, and later spawned a wide range of popular literature and manga on the evil doings of daughters-in-law.
16 *Oniyome Nikki* was first broadcast by Fuji TV in 2005, starring Japanese actress Mikuza Arisa and actor Gori. Fuji TV broadcast the sequel *Oniyome Nikki II Yudana*, featuring the same lead actor and actress, in 2007.
17 The popularity of the first series *Oniyome Nikki* spawned a wide range of popular literature and *manga* (Japanese comics), including *Tomizu Ken's Diary About His Wife* (2008), *True Accounts of the Demonic Daughter-in-Law* (Ozaki 2005) and two volumes of comics entitled *True Accounts of the Demonic Daughter-in-Law* (Ozaki 2006a, 2006b).
18 Empress Dowager Cixi (1835–1908) is popularly known in China as the West Empress Dowager, who was the de facto ruler of the Manchu or Qing Dynasty in China for 47 years between 1861 and 1908. It was during her reign when the three

Anglo-Chinese Opium Wars took place, which eventually forced China to open up many ports across the country to various European powers. Empress Dowager Cixi is also widely known for her cruelty towards various other concubines, and for ruling China using a child emperor.

19 While the term *baito* is more generally used to refer to the irregular jobs of young high school and college students, many married and older women in Japan would also use it to describe their part-time work.

20 This reference is used to describe a woman for having passed her marriageable age or expiry date at 25 years (Brinton 1992).

21 Nikkei Woman is a monthly magazine published by one of Japan's largest publishing company Nihon Keizai Shimbun.

22 The explanation in Japanese was '*josei ga shakai ni dete hataraku koto no sukunai jidai ni shokugyō wo motsu shakai ni dete hataraku katsudō teki na josei.*'

23 Nakane Chie's (1967, 1970) works, particularly *Tateshakai on Ningen Kankei* (Human Relations in a Vertical Society) portrayed Japan as a naturally group-oriented but also harmonious society, though primarily to justify the highly hierarchical structure of Japanese corporations. Doi Takeo (1971, 1973, 1986) was known for his book *Amae no Kōzō* (Anatomy of Dependence) in which the psychologist explained 'groupism' in Japan as an important and necessary means for bonding between workers, and between employers and employees.

24 This view was strongly expounded by psychologist Kawai Hayao (1976: 24–8) in his book *Bosei Shakai Nihon no Byōri* (The Pathology of Japan as a Maternal Society).

25 Motherhood for Japanese women was systemically enforced by the Meiji government through the introduction of the *ie* system and implementation of the Confucian feminine ideal of *ryōsai kenbo* in the Civil Code in 1896 to promote nationalism and modernization (Ho 2018: 21–2; Mackie 2003). Together, these measures enshrined patriarchy as the norm for all Japanese families and imposed the sexual division of labour in Japanese society by assigning women to the 'private world of the home' and men to the public domain of paid work (Uno 1993: 296–7).

26 The Japanese word *shakai* means 'society,' and *jin* means 'a person' or 'people.'

27 The Equal Employment Opportunity Law (*Danjo Koyō Byōdōhō*), which came into effect on 1 April 1986, applies to all employees – generally referred to as *sōgō shoku* (comprehensive employees) – and requires all companies to include male and female employees in their system of lifetime employment and seniority-based promotions (Molony 1995: 286; Ōwaki 1987: 229).

28 The Nikkei stock price average on the Tokyo Stock Exchange plunged by 63.2 per cent, from 38915.9 on 29 December 1989 to 14309.4 on 18 August 1992.

29 After the notion of *make inu* became a media sensation, it generated a wide range of scholarly debates and public forums, especially in popular literature and comics even today (for more discussions on the topic, see Kumazawa 2002; Shimizu 2005; Yamazaki 2006).

30 The term *furītā* in Japanese combines the English word 'free' with the German word *arbeit* or 'work' to refer to people in temporary, contingent jobs (Roberts 2005: 113).

31 The term *nītto* came from NEET first used by the UK government to classify a growing number of people who were 'Not in Education, Employment or Training,' and emerged in Japan during the 2000s (Hamada 2005: 136).

32 Former health minister Yanagisawa Hakuo made the speech at the Liberal Democratic Party's assembly in Matsue in Shimane Prefecture on 27 January 2007 (Ito 2007).

3 In the company of co-workers

Performing gender and drinking for survival

Sasaki Shiori has been a vegetarian and a teetotaller for many years, even though she has long recovered from gastro-intestinal and skin problems caused by heavy drinking. Her employer was compassionate enough to allow her ample leave to seek medical treatment in the past, even though there is no statutory sick leave and the company does not provide any for employees. Her superiors have also been understanding, and have factored in her health conditions in several annual performance appraisals. But Sasaki was taken aback one day when she was asked to consider stepping down from her former senior management position as Business Development Team Leader, and moving to another division to assume the role of Manager of Customer Support. She was told, albeit unofficially, that her ability to lead her team has been undermined by her prolonged ill health and her inability to drink. These have prevented Sasaki from leading and participating in important drinking activities with co-workers, business associates, and potential clients. Her team had also not performed as well as others. Her staying on as team leader would jeopardize her subordinates' job performance. She is still puzzled by the employer's explanation, wondering how her ability to drink and entertain which had once lifted her up the corporate ladder to become the first woman in the company to lead a business development team – a position for which she had worked hard to secure since joining the company in the early 2000s – had also become the very cause of her health complications and her career descent.

Sasaki agreed to the demotion and transfer after a night out with her team of eight subordinates who had beseeched her as *onēsan* (older sister) to understand their predicaments, and to help them keep their job by working under a different team leader. Sasaki has trained countless subordinates during the 12 years with this European company. Two permanent employees had one day addressed her as *onēsan*, perhaps as a way of showing their appreciation for the divorcee's caring attitude towards them and the other eight part-time members of their team. Sasaki was initially uncomfortable with the fictive kin address, though she gradually grew accustomed to it. Her promotion to team leader had incurred the envy and dissatisfaction of several peers, though she earned it through many years of hard work to excel in her job performance. She set aside time and her own money to acquire new professional qualifications, and also attended weekend classes to improve on her command of English. In addition to purchasing and subscribing to a wide range of materials to stay abreast of the latest developments in financial regulations and business trends, Sasaki also went out regularly to drink with her team, and paid for their exorbitant nights out from her own pocket which could easily cost 30,000 yen ($276, or £228) per evening. The 51-year-old would also spend a considerable sum each month on sampling a large variety of alcoholic beverages – from *nihonshu* (Japanese rice wine) and *shōchū* (alcoholic drink brewed from root vegetables), to wine, champagne, and a variety of liquor and spirits – as a form of professional education that would help with business entertainment and negotiations.

What used to be a team of 13 permanent workers during her early days with the company was gradually transformed into one comprising only three full-time employees and eight part-time workers on short-term contracts. With a shrinking staff training budget and a growing lack of commitment on the part of the part-time workers to their job, the team's weekly drinking sessions were critical for Sasaki to train her subordinates, boost their morale, and forge a semblance of team bonding in the hope of improving the team's performance and also of enhancing her image as team leader. Despite all this, she was only regarded as *onēsan*, unlike several of her male peers who were more respectfully addressed by their own subordinates with professional references, such as *kachō* (head of a sub-division), *kanrikan* (manager), boss, or leader.

Sasaki cut back on the drinking gatherings after she was forced by her illness to go on a strict non-alcoholic and vegetarian diet. She was not only kept out of the loop on the latest gossips and useful information circulating within the office, but she also gradually lost the loyalty of several subordinates who had shifted allegiance to be friendly with other team leaders. Determined to regain their loyalty and re-affirm her authority as team leader, Sasaki resumed the regular after-work gatherings with her team, though she would pace herself over her drinks. When necessary, she would take over some unfinished tasks assigned to her subordinates, especially the part-time workers, and work late at home to complete them. Furthermore, Sasaki continued to spend a considerable amount of her monthly income on sampling new brands and varieties of alcoholic beverages, as well as building up her home library of magazines and books on food and beverages.

Performing the role of *onēsan* gradually became a necessary and crucial strategy for Sasaki to keep her job, maintain her position of authority, and hopefully also improve her prospects of getting another promotion. Like many women managers in Japan, Sasaki too has changed jobs frequently during the early 1990s before finding a full-time position. Her biggest, if not the only, hope today is to remain in employment at the same workplace until she retires. At 51 years of age, Sasaki knows that her chances of securing a job elsewhere with a similar level in salary and responsibilities are very slim. As many of my informants have said, Sasaki knows that women aged 40 years and above are perceived by employers as *toshi-sugi* (too old), *taka-sugi* (too expensive), and *era-sugi* (too superior in position). They are less desirable in contrast to younger female workers who would and could work harder for a lesser pay. Sasaki has once assumed that she would be better off working in a European company than a conservative Japanese one, but was later disappointed to note that conservatism is deeply rooted in the attitude of many Japanese people wherever they work. If performing the role of a caring *onēsan* should gain her respect as a manager, help mitigate her own sense of job insecurity, and perhaps also protect her job, Sasaki would gladly accept it and try to excel in this traditional gender role despite it being incongruous with her identity as a professionally qualified and capable corporate executive. Others might find her less threatening than an aggressive or ambitious career woman, since she is after all performing a role that women are 'naturally' expected to do (Borovoy 2005; Hochschild 1983). As Sasaki explains to me one day:

> It is sad that I need to be reduced to a mere *onēsan* in order to be respected as a manager, but what choice do I have? Women do not have as many opportunities as men have to enhance their professional image legitimately. While we need to accept our position of inferiority, we must also do all we can to utilize the appropriate means that could help us stay within the system and benefit from it.

Since transferring to customer services, Sasaki is still required to go out drinking with co-workers and pay for their share (partially or fully) at her own expense on her reduced salary and inferior managerial position. What she finds most unbearable is having to live with the title of *onēsan*, which her current superior had once remarked as 'the perfect description' for a mature, caring, and responsible customer services personnel such as Sasaki.

From forging corporate identity to protecting one's job

Sasaki is among countless adults in Japan for whom drinking is an important part of their working life. They have long been prepared while attending universities, where clubs and societies often organize drinking activities for members. Drinking is encouraged by employers as a means of forging stronger bonds among workers, who themselves also regard drinking as necessary for establishing social networks and important connections to enhance their career prospects, and for alleviating work-related stress outside the office and the home (Atsumi 1979; Befu 1986; Takada 1983). Drinking in Japan has been described as marking an important symbolic passage 'from serious to the playful; from predictable order to risky role-release' for working adults, and as 'fun time' that is 'opposite in quality and style to the serious activities of life' (Gusfield 1987: 84). Alcohol consumption is also said to inject a degree of play to balance out the seriousness of work and enhance workers' productivity (Allison 1994; Ben-Ari 2002; Hendry 1997; Linhart 1998; Valentine 1990). Japanese workers across the country participate in several big drinking parties every year, especially for *shinnenkai* (New Year's party) at the beginning of the calendar year, *hanami* (cherry-blossom viewing) in springtime, *hanabi* (fireworks) in the summer, and *bōnenkai* (year-end party) in December. During the bubble decade when corporations' entertainment expenses were endorsed by the state way of tax rebates, drinking so was widely projected as a symbolic of corporate masculinity for white-collar male workers to forge stronger bonds among themselves and enhance the corporate identity of their respective employers that corporate work and drinking among *sararīman* had been referred to as the 'Siamese twins of Japanese welfare capitalism' (Moeran 1998: 243).

Even today, drinking is still regarded a necessity for working adults to enhance *nomunikēshon*[1] (romanized from 'nomunication' which means 'drinking communication') for establishing better relations and forming important social networks. However, the significance of drinking has shifted from being symbolic of corporate identity and for the benefit of a collective, to that of individual self-interest and for the survival of the individual in the corporate world. While drinking among workers continues to be encouraged by employers too, tax rebates on corporate entertainment have vanished since the demise of bubble economy, and the growing number of white-collar workers on short-term employment contracts is today no longer able to form their identity in relation to their employer. Other than high-level executives with corporate credit cards, most white-collar workers drink at their own expense.

There is also another shift in the symbolic meaning and practice of drinking for corporate workers. As *tenshoku* replaces permanent employment as the dominant work norm, it weakens the bonds among workers and those between employers and employees. With more corporate employees being hired as irregular workers on part-time or short-term contracts, the importance of drinking as enhancing solidarity among workers comprising many who are constantly moving from job to job is mainly for a short duration or the immediate present, and not for establishing long-term bonds. Meanwhile, the increasing lack of *ibasho* (sense of belonging in a workplace) renders employee relations unstable and disharmonious, and the task of managing employees in a workplace with high staff turnover demanding and difficult. Drinking among workers hence increases in importance as a tool for survival and coping with the growing precarious conditions of one's job.

Yet, one symbolic significance of drinking remains little changed. The rapid expansion of Japan's female corporate workforce since the 1980s has permitted many women to cross the private–public divide and gain greater access to corporate work and management-track careers. This has also enabled them to appropriate this once male-dominated practice and legitimize drinking as an important part of their working life. However, drinking has never been associated with femininity in Japan, nor has its symbolic significance with salaried work for women (Ho 2018: 35). And while women's enhanced economic position has prompted brewers and entertainment establishments to target white-collar female workers as customers and expand their market to include women, the commercially driven changes are yet to translate directly into a greater social acceptance of drinking for women (Ho 2015). It is more common to find working women in Japan who drink portrayed in media discourses and scholarly works as alcoholics (Higuchi et al. 2007; Ito 2014; Takano et al. 1996), for their inability to cope with the stresses and demands of working life (Gotoh 1989: 953; Hendry 1997: 187), than as modern individuals with desires for cosmopolitan consumption or as independent professionals whose lifestyle includes drinking (Ho 2015: 41–2, 2018: 40). A less discussed and more pertinent issue is their increased risk of developing drinking-related problems, which may adversely affect their career prospects, or even end their professional career, as in the case of Sasaki.

Strategizing from the peripheries of Japan's corporate world

Mother in the office

For many women managers in this study, their career would be in jeopardy if they do not negotiate delicately and adeptly the contradictory and conflicting perceptions of women who drink, together with the necessity of drinking. Among several common strategies that some women adopt is by way of gender role performance, as Sasaki has done, at times by enacting gender stereotypes imposed on them by others, and in other cases willingly conforming to established norms. While this does not always lead to desirable consequences, appealing to cultural stereotypes by performing socially acceptable roles expected of women is a convenient – though ironic – way of managing their identity as highly educated, professionally qualified, confident and capable executives in the gendered corporate workplace. Doing so certainly highlights the limitations that many women experience as non-core players and marginalized subjects, and perhaps also reinforce their peripheral role. Yet, at the same time, these strategies also provide a means of turning themselves into empowered individuals, at least to themselves if not also to others.

Kizaki Kazumi has two children and is thus not unfamiliar with the role of a mother. The 46-year-old has been balancing the demands of her job as Human Resource Director and the responsibilities of motherhood since joining a small American company in Tokyo. She lives in a large house in a posh, upper-middle-class Tokyo district where she has her own study room which her husband and two children refer to as 'The Chairman's Office' (in English). She also has an equitable arrangement with her husband – a senior banker – by splitting the domestic chores, household expenses, and caring for their two children, though with the aid of a *herupa-san* (domestic helper).

Since the couple gives their children a lot of autonomy, the latter have been well-trained to do their share of housework and do not need much supervision when it comes to schoolwork. During the several weeks that I stayed with the family, I also observed how her husband and children would not only leave Kizaki undisturbed in 'The Chairman's Office' whenever she had unfinished work to do after returning home, but they would at times serve her tea and snacks when she remained in her study room till very late.

In the office, however, Kizaki's image is reversed. The head of human resource has no office of her own. Her desk is a corner end space of a long fixture shared by eight employees. For reasons she still cannot remember, Kizaki somehow earned the nickname *ofisu no okāsan*[2] (mother in the office) many years ago. Perhaps it was the patience she has shown in listening to others, appeasing their frustrations, managing their disappointment, and ironing out differences between employees. I have heard new employees refer to and address Kizaki as *okāsan* on the several occasions when I went out drinking with the Human Resource Director and her subordinates. Even her superiors have teasingly complimented her for playing the role of a mother well, and told her 'Good job!' Despite resenting the incongruity of the image of 'mother' to her education, intelligence, and professional capabilities, Kizaki eventually made herself appreciate some of its 'benefits.' After all, Japan is said to be a *bosei shakai* (maternal society) where the mother figure supposedly commands respect and admiration from both men and women (Kawai 1976; Yoda 2006).

Kizaki was surprised to observe how more employees became more willing to take orders from her as a mother figure than as a female superior, which gradually elevated her status over and above the powers and responsibilities that she actually possessed. The job of the human resource division of a company is typically viewed as a back-office operation involving the processing of paperwork on the hiring, promoting, transferring, paying, appraising, and firing of employees based on decisions made by upper management, with the head of personnel occasionally exerting a little influence. As word began to spread in the office that Kizaki's power of persuasion and 'soft approach' as a caring yet firm mother figure have earned her the trust and respect from her superiors, more employees started confiding in her, informing her of internal strife, intra-office romance, gossips, and various other problems. This, in turn, strengthened Kizaki's power of influence and also her symbolic stature, and transformed her image from that of a mere paper-pusher. Yet, the mother of two still does not feel secure about her job, since human resource is a woman's job which can easily be undertaken by any female employee with sufficient skills and experience. As she explains:

> I often think that I have wasted a lot of my time and my parents' money attending university to get a good education, when I could have started working much earlier. No, I would need to be a mother first and then get a job.

> A woman's place in the corporate world is an extremely fragile one. Good opportunities do not come often. All the talk about individual freedom and equality is mere rhetoric, used by the powerful to maintain their positions of power. The weak must seek therefore their own ways to improve their conditions and gain the power they are not given.

But Kizaki realizes that the price she is paying for enduring the unprofessional reference far surpasses the respect and trust that she gains as a mother figure, and can at times be unbearable. To begin with, managing the personnel matters of a company with nearly a hundred employees is by no means an easy feat. Conflicts and disputes often arise over promotions, salary levels, bonuses, job transfers, recruitment, and retrenchment. From several after-work gatherings she had with her co-workers, I observed how this *kaisha de no okāsan* had to listen to complaints about job dissatisfaction; manage workers' feelings of insecurity, discontentment, anxieties, and frustrations; and entertain requests for internal transfers, higher salaries, and better work assignments. Most matters are beyond her authority, though Kizaki has to carefully manage her image and give the impression that she has done her very best to negotiate on each of their behalf but failed. When that happens, Kizaki would try to appease her co-workers' anger or disappointment by taking them out to dinner and buying them drinks at her own expense. Given that her employer has made it a regular practice to reduce the corporate staff budget every quarter, she would be out drinking with co-workers four to five nights a week every three months to manage her team's morale. As the bill of an evening of meals and drinks could easily amount to 30,000 yen ($276, or £228), this means that Kizaki would spend at least 600,000 yen ($5,520, or £4,560) a year on after-work drinking with her co-workers. Fortunately, the physically exhausted and emotionally drained Kizaki has 'The Chairman's Office' to retire to after reaching home where she would quietly sip a few glasses of her favourite red wine on her own to unwind before bed.

A pretty, sexy girl should not work too hard

Like Sasaki and Kizaki, several other women managers in this study also have to endure the enactment of unflattering gender roles that place them in a conflicting and ambivalent position. Forty-six-year-old Miura Miho is someone who knows this fairly well. Miura was working for a multinational American consultancy firm in Tokyo when I first knew her in the late 2000s, though she is currently employed elsewhere. Since she was promoted to be leader of a team of market consultants at 28 years of age, Miura became the target of harsh criticisms and vicious gossips in the consultancy firm. She had heard co-workers and subordinates express doubts about whether this married but childless woman with no experience in looking after children was capable of managing a team of eight, five of whom were older in age and possess more years of experience in the business. Others had insinuated that this pretty *sararī gāru* (salaried girl) was promoted ahead of some others because of her good looks, or that she had slept with one or more male bosses.

Miura was also teased for being an *ojōsan* (young lady, usually from an upper-class background) whose capabilities and value to the company were recognized due to the potential business connections that could be offered by her father, an influential banker, and her husband, a well-known lawyer and businessman. On occasions when Miura had clinched a lucrative business contract, word spread like wildfire in the office that she had yet again closed a deal because of her father or her husband, or worse, that she had exchanged sex to obtain them. Being tall, slim, and well-dressed, Miura often received compliments on her being pretty and sexy, and had also been told that she could be an excellent and popular hostess club's *mama-san* (literally 'mother,' a term of reference for women who manage hostess clubs and entertainment venues for men). While she had also been called *bābī*[3] (Barbie doll) along with several other less flattering descriptions of good-looking women as stupid, Miura was stuck with the nickname *gāru* (girl) till the day she left her former workplace.

Despite having graduated from one of Japan's top ten universities and excelling in school, Miura was often complimented for her slender body and good looks by colleagues and business clients. Being teased as *gāru* had bothered her, though she later tried to use it to her advantage, especially to massage the egos of some difficult male co-workers who had refused to view her as a figure of authority, and to reduce their antagonism towards her. The office culture was predominantly Japanese and male. Out of the total of 40 employees, five were foreigners and 11 women. All the female employees were in administrative, clerical, and secretarial positions, except for a junior supervisor and Miura, who was the only female divisional head.

To work well with her co-workers, Miura often went out drinking with them and soon became adept at performing the role of *gāru*. As I observed from several nights out with Miura and her subordinates, the team leader would typically accept a challenge to drink as many rounds of liqueur shots as she could, though she would readily admit defeat when she noticed that a male colleague had reached his limit. She would then apologize profusely for being a *gāru* who could not hold her drink, and complimented the male subordinate for being a good drinker. At times, after her male colleagues were pleased to have won the drinking games, Miura would play the less experienced and knowledgeable *gāru* and sought their opinions and advice on certain work matters. Being a *gāru* meant performing the role of a woman and an inferior. Employing this skilfully helped Miura alter her subordinates' attitude towards her as a non-threatening team leader, persuading them also to willingly offer assistance to her in the office. The task of managing thus became less demanding as Miura dealt with less opposition, conflicts, stress, and frustrations. As she explains to me over a dinner I had with her alone one day:

> People could call me whatever they like. I am happy so long as I can do my job without too many unnecessary obstacles. I could quit at any time

> if I wanted to, and I did really want to do so many times. But I am not working for money. I stayed in the company because I knew I was good at my job, and that made me feel good about myself. If it took enduring all the nicknames to allow me to prove myself, then it was worth it.
>
> Women are always given unflattering nicknames anyway. Being seen as a *garū* was not too bad. It made me feel young, beautiful, and attractive…at least that was how I tried to comfort myself. It could have been worse, for example, to be called *baba* (middle-aged or older woman) or a bitch…
>
> (*laughs*)

Miura would not have quit had the company's managing director not complained that she had worked too hard and performed too well that she had embarrassed other team leaders – all male – who complained that they were given unfair appraisals due to Miura's 'special business connections' which had contributed to her good work performance. She was one day called into the managing director's office, and was told to not work too hard *(ganbaranakute iiyo*), to pass some of the deals that she had clinched to the others, and to let 'the boys' outshine her from time to time. It shocked her to know that excelling well in her work and outperforming other teams could be causes for poor work appraisal. What shocked her more, and probably infuriated her enough to tender her resignation, were his following words: 'Why would a pretty, sexy and rich girl like you want to work so hard for?'

Miura currently works as Senior Marketing Consultant in a European firm, where she is no longer called a *gāru*. It would be odd to be called one, since she is now in her mid-forties. Looking back, she often wonders how she had endured the teasing. She sometimes prides herself for how well she had managed her bruised ego and self-esteem during those nine years at her former workplace. Too bad that the soon-to-be implemented law[4] on *pawahara* (power harassment) and corporate bullying should come this late. She could have filed legal suits against various people in her former company back then, Miura said to me with a hearty laugh when I met her recently. Putting up with the derogatory references to her as *garū*, *ojōsan*, and *bābī* might have been more bearable if she could at times also be recognized as someone who was *shigoto ga jōzu* (good at her work), or *atama ga ii* (intelligent). Being a product of the 'neoliberal turn' in Japan when she had been taught to pursue *jibunrashī seikatsu* (a lifestyle of one's own) and seek *jūjitsukan* (self-fulfilment) based on her own capabilities, Miura has found reality to be contrary to all the discourses she had been trained to embrace in school. Women's paths to *jikohakken* (self-realization) could never be similar to those of Japanese men's in the corporate world. Even with regard to social drinking, which is widely considered acceptable for working adults in Japan, women are more closely scrutinized for how, what, where, and how much they drink. Japanese men, however, are subject to less ridicule and criticisms. Though a good drinker herself, Miura still has to be cautious about the pace and amount of alcohol she consumes when she drinks with co-workers, since she could no longer enact the cultural stereotype of *gāru* as a survival strategy for a woman her age, and would hence be more harshly evaluated.

It is not uncommon for women to enact prevailing gender roles as tactics to improve their conditions in a gendered work environment in Japan (Kondo 1990; Ogasawara 1998; Roberts 2005), or for marginalized individuals to appeal to cultural stereotypes to change their oppressed situations elsewhere (Kim 2004; Ortner 1999; Spivak 1988). From blue-collar factory workers in a large garment manufacturing company in Kansai, to part-time female factory workers in a small artisan factory in Tokyo, and women doing secretarial and administrative work in a bank in Tokyo, many women have been documented in studies as appealing to what Dorinne K. Kondo (1990: 298–9) described as 'culturally appropriate meanings of gender' to deal with the various contradictions between traditional socio-cultural ideologies and modern economic reality, resist being marginalized, and even turn them into central figures in the workplace.

Living up to male ideals

Japanese men too have their fair share of difficulties and conflicts in the workplace, particularly those in managerial positions who do not drink and those who cannot hold their drink. Men may not have the same 'privilege' as women to mobilize feminine stereotypes to enhance their work conditions, but the challenges for some could be demoralizing and demeaning. From several interviews I had with white-collar male workers, I learned that they have been ridiculed as *otoko janai* (not men, or unmasculine), *onna poi* (like a woman, or feminine), *yowai* (weak), and even *tsukaenai* (useless). What these suggest is that gender role expectations – especially gender polarization – continue to be deeply embedded in Japanese society even today, despite the neoliberal educational reforms and increased cosmopolitanism over the past decades. In the corporate workplace, men are under more intense pressure to live up to conventional perceptions of masculinity than women, for the obvious reason that it is a predominantly male domain.

I have seen a former colleague of mine Kimura Kotaro being teased frequently for being a *kodomo* (child) for drinking non-alcoholic beverages whenever we went out after work. He could, and in fact liked, to drink. But his face would instantly turn red after a sip of beer that he lied about being a teetotaller to save him from being ridiculed, as he was at his first workplace. But consuming only soft drinks in the company of co-workers was also problematic. The then 30-year-old sales supervisor was often embarrassed, especially at my former workplace where the Sales Manager had loudly laugh at Kimura for being a *yowai otoko* (weak man). Perhaps his boss had acted out of compassion by passing all assignments that required entertaining and negotiating with clients to Kimura's peer who was more sociable, but Kimura was quick to realize that his career prospects as an *eigyōman*[5] (salesman, to mean a man working in sales) in the company were dim, and hence resigned after working for two years.

The importance of drinking for Japanese men is less about forging bonding with their fellow workers as it is about living up to expectations of what it means to be masculine in Japan. Since drinking is an essential part of his job, it is hence critical for a man to maintain his masculine identity. Such a view seems to have remained little changed over the years. Recently, one informant's husband Tanaka Takeo nearly missed the arrival of his first born when he failed to excuse himself from a drinking session with co-workers and clients. He wanted to witness the baby's arrival after his wife went into labour. However, his superior chided him for not knowing his priorities, and for jeopardizing his position as manager for making such a request, adding that good permanent jobs were scarce and that he was easily replaceable. Tanaka joined the drinking gathering, but for several hours and then rushed to the hospital. He arrived several minutes before his child was born. Tanaka asked for his boss to approve several days of paternity leave the next day, and was chided again for wishing to do such an 'unmanly act.' He withdrew the request, fearing that his position might not be there for him to return to after his leave. What confused Tanaka was that the company policy offered male employees rather generous paternity leave, but some members of the senior management would exert pressure on workers to not utilize it. Tanaka had heard and read many news reports on men being 'punished' in various ways for taking paternity leave. Now that there was an extra mouth to feed, he could not afford to lose his position or job. The corporate policy is said to not be for enforcement, but a mere paper to show investors and the government of the company's compliance with a good business practice.

The gendered corporate workplace reflects the gender polarization in the broader Japanese society, where it is difficult for both women and men to avoid being perceived and evaluated based on prevailing gender role expectations. Despite calls by the government for corporations to allow employees a better work-life balance in corporate policies, a lack of mandatory enforcement or monitoring by the state of actual practices in the workplace renders many measures ineffective and futile. Take paternity leave provision, for instance. Until today, policymakers and lawmakers are still debating over whether or not to make paternity leave mandatory, despite repeated rhetoric on its potential benefit of encouraging childbirths to resolve some of the country's problems relating to declining birth rates and an ageing population (Ji 2019; Shirakawa 2019; Shoji 2019).

According to a report published by United Nations Children's Fund (UNICEF 2019: 10), Japan is said to offer the longest paternity leave among OECD countries of up to 30 weeks, but only 5.14 per cent of eligible fathers took paid leave in 2017, a meagre increase from 1.56 per cent a decade earlier in 2007. A survey conducted by UNICEF showed that 45 per cent of male employees on regular contracts with children under 3 did not want to take the leave, while another 35 per cent would like to use the paternity leave but could not do so, due to reasons such as understaffing, 'unfavourable atmosphere,' workload, pay loss, and career impediment (Ibid.). Many white-collar male workers, like Tanaka, have given me similar explanations for not taking paternity leave, feeling compelled to conform to certain expectations of male ideals, which some described as a powerful means for people in senior positions to force workers to serve the interests of corporations, and not really to uphold traditional Japanese values. One ideal which Tanaka believes to be enduring and difficult for men to disregard is the perception of the *ii otōsan* (good father) in Japan as a man who is capable of providing financially for his family, and not the one who devotes time and attention to his wife and children.

A female breadwinner as a father figure

Tanaka's remark points to the sexual division of labour formalized in the Civil Code of 1896 by the Meiji government by mobilizing the ideology of *kazoku kokka* (the state as family) to establish *ie* (the household) as the foundation of the state (Mackie 2003: 21). The socio-historical construction of gender in Japan has since relegated men to the public realm of paid work, and women to the private sphere of domesticity. Economic contingencies may have since then necessitated the expansion of the country's female workforce, but Japanese men's role as the main economic provider of the family is yet to dissipate. The postwar gender ideals of the *sararīman* for men and *sengyō shufu* for women are not radically different from the Meiji ideals of men as *iemoto* (head of a household) and women as *ryōsai kenbo* (Good Wives Wise Mothers) (White 2002: 126; Yoda 2006: 247). The fact that this bifurcation of individuals into gender stereotypes still persists today means that men and women are constantly caught within the polarized standards of masculinity and femininity. This is perhaps why women who have entered the predominantly male realm of salaried work are sometimes perceived as emulating the male behaviour. Whether it is the way they work, perform a task, drink, or smoke, some of my informants have had their behaviour described as *otoko mitai* (like a man), and several have even performed the enactment of male roles.

Gohara Kozue is rare among my informants in that she was given the nicknames *iemoto*, and *otōsan* (father) in the office. Till today, she still could not recall when or how that happened. Perhaps it was the knowledge about her being the sole breadwinner of a family of five that Gohara gained the respect of her co-workers and superiors, and hence the nickname *iemoto*. Her boldness to stand up to her superiors and insist on a particular course of action that she knows to be good for the company led her immediate superior to liken her to a father, which also earned her the nickname *otōsan*.

Gohara had thought it would be fleeting, but it became permanent. Worse, her colleagues seemed to be serious and respectful in using the nicknames, and not out of spite. It was all rather fuzzy, she said. One thing was certain. She was befuddled, and had felt extremely uncomfortable with both nicknames for years. As she explained:

> Am I living in the 21st century? Who are these people? Am I working in an office? Why is this bunch of modern, educated people behaving as if they are in the past, or in some backward, rural community? First of all, I am not a man. Secondly, the office is not my home nor are the workers my family. More importantly, I am a professionally qualified accountant, and not a manager of a household…

For Gohara, being called *iemoto* and *otōsan* is not only incongruous with her being Deputy Head of Finance, but *iemoto* is an old-fashioned word which depicts hierarchy, inequality, and oppression, which aptly depict the structure of Japanese society. *Otōsan* is the modern terminology of the old *iemoto*, a figure of supreme authority within a household or organization, as the grand masters of some traditional Japanese cultural practices of tea ceremony, music, dance, and calligraphy are still being referred to today (Chiba 2011: 10). He is also a figure of stability, protection, wisdom, and responsibility, for ensuring the continuity of the institution that he represents by producing heirs, and grooming apprentices or disciples. Gohara's diligence and cautious approach to investing funds, managing debts, and negotiating with creditors have saved her employer several times from financial difficulties during recent economic crises. She is also perceived as a good mentor to junior co-workers, both regular and irregular employees.

Despite possessing all the qualities of an ideal Japanese father or head of a household, the mother of two thinks that she has not been well treated by her employer. The three promotions she was given since joining the company in the early 2000s had each come with a change in job title and increased responsibilities, but a long delay in salary increment. Even then, the total pay increase from all the promotions was so little that she actually experienced a real cut in her overall salary from the time when the word 'manager' was not on her business card. Since becoming Assistant Manager, she supposedly became a member of the management team, and is by law no longer entitled to overtime pay.[6] Her working hours lengthened after the promotion, but they were all *sābisu zangyō*[7] (free overtime). Gohara failed on numerous attempts to persuade her superiors for a raise, and came very close to quitting her job on several occasions. The fear of landing herself in a new job with lesser pay prevented her from switching jobs. As the real *iemoto* in the home, Gohara needs a good, regular source of income to meet the medical expenses for her husband and mother-in-law, and also to provide for her children's education. Like most women managers in Japan who are aged 50 years and older, Gohara is not confident that she is able to find another job that would maintain her present financial situation. She has little choice but to trust her superiors who repeatedly assure Gohara that she could continue working for the company till she retires. In the meantime, she has to put up with being addressed as *otōsan*, and occasionally also as *iemoto-sama* (*sama* being a suffix to show respect when addressing someone), roles which she seems to perform exceedingly well on the few occasions when I went out drinking with Gohara and her colleagues.

Gohara usually drinks with her team every Friday after work, though not all the eight workers would be present. I was fortunate to meet the entire team one evening in 2018. The atmosphere was tense when I arrived. I soon learned that the accounting supervisor Yamada Yasuo would have lost his job had Gohara not fought hard for him. Yamada had made several wrong accounting entries that led the external auditors to suspect the company of doing something illegal. The errors had been rectified and the company cleared of any suspicion, but all members of the board were so embarrassed and infuriated that they ordered Yamada to resign with immediate effect. Gohara had pleaded to the board to understand that she and Yamada had worked overtime for several months, and that the errors were due to exhaustion and fatigue. The finance team had shrunk in size over the years that there were only three full-time employees, including Gohara as head, and five part-timers. The finance team could not perform all the monthly, quarterly, and annual accounting tasks without this capable and efficient employee whom Gohara had depended on for more than eight years. Gohara was praised for fighting hard to protect her team member, as she was said to have negotiated to extend the employment contracts of all the part-time workers on her team. Gohara would cover for them when they needed to take an urgent leave. She would help them improve on their accounting knowledge even though the part-timers would not stay long on the team, and at times Gohara had also lent money to a few to help them make payments for rent or utilities. One part-time worker had this to say:

> Gohara *fukubuchō* (the deputy head) is very protective and caring. She fights for all of us, and will not give up until she gets the company to approve what she thinks is the right thing to do. She really lives up to her nicknames as *otōsan* and *iemoto*, though she could have done more if she was a man…

Gohara had blushed as her team members continued to shower her with praises. Her cheeks reddened again when we talked about that evening several weeks later, when she also shared her thoughts on why she continues to drink with her subordinates every week. The company has been intensifying its efforts to cut staff cost by shrinking inefficient divisions and firing unproductive employees. Gohara would thus like to help her subordinates as much as she could, even though it is exhausting. The part-time workers come and go so often that she constantly needs to maintain a steady level of productivity within her team by going out drinking with them. Her image and status as a good manager would otherwise be at stake. But paying for the nights out on her reduced salary is exerting a lot of pressure on her own financial position, especially given the heavy family commitments that she is bearing.

Yet, at the same time, she also feels sorry for her subordinates. The two regular employees are in their mid- to late forties, and are unlikely to find a better job elsewhere. Many of the irregular employees are divorced single mothers who have drifted from job to job for so long that they probably could never find a permanent position anywhere. Gohara could only encourage and teach them a little more about accounting in the hope of improving their prospects of securing better part-time positions, though she also derives comfort from their companionship. After all, they are all – including Gohara herself – dispensable workers in an environment where employers cared little about the welfare of employees. Perhaps it is the lack of a sense of belonging and purpose they experience that Gohara could gain her subordinates' appreciation and respect as some kind of a father figure. The fact that the finance team is managed well under Gohara's leadership has also earned her the trust of her superiors to handle more responsible and confidential tasks, even though her own position in the medium-sized trading company confers neither prestige nor power. She is thus resigned to being a *ko-iemoto* (little head of the household) of her tiny team, and a convenient father figure in managing tasks for the company's benefits, hoping that this could allow her to keep the job that she badly needs.

Drinking and working like a man

It is not common for women managers to perform a male role or to emulate a male figure, since the majority of female corporate executives tend to work in feminine types of work such as finance, administration, public relations, corporate communications, and human resource management. However, there are cases when women holding supervisory or managerial positions in lines of work that are predominantly male are treated, or required to behave, like men. Umeda Yoriko is one of them. The 48-year-old single woman is in a slightly different line of work from Gohara, being the only female to take charge of a sales team of 14 young, ambitious, and aggressive men, and three female in supporting roles. As Sales and Marketing Director, Umeda's behaviour and work performance within the historically male domain are closely scrutinized and monitored by her superiors, peers, and subordinates. Umeda realizes over the years that it is difficult for her to appeal to culturally constituted perceptions of femininity in her daily interactions with co-workers and business clients, as these would be construed as signs of weakness and incompetence for an *eigyōman*. Instead, she has to be and look 'as tough as a man,' in order to succeed and manage male subordinates who do not submit readily to a female superior. For this reason, Umeda has not worn a skirt or dress for more than 20 years. She is always immaculately attired in a fashionable pantsuit in plain colours, keeps her hair short, and wears minimal makeup. She drinks beer mostly, and chain smokes like the men in her family.

Since a person's competence in corporate sales is measured in terms of charisma, audacity, and the ability to drink, Umeda would prove her abilities to her subordinates. Sociable and charismatic, Umeda could out-talk any of her subordinated in terms of speed, and easily win an argument. Having trained herself to be a good drinker, she could out-drink all her male subordinates in terms of speed and the volume of alcohol consumed. But she would manage her pace and alcohol intake adeptly. As I have observed from more than ten drinking sessions that I participated in, Umeda would often initiate and accept a challenge to drink, usually over a word game, puzzle, or riddle. Whether someone wins or loses, both parties have to quickly empty their glasses of beer. Umeda rarely loses, though she would occasionally pretend to when she thinks a subordinate needs to win, or when the latter has lost enough. After all, the sales job is about winning, and every single member of her team needs to feel and think that he or she is a winner. She would also treat her subordinates generously to meals and drinks. When her team has won a sales contract or achieved a good sales target, the night out would be a very long one that sometimes end in the early hours of the morning. She would not hesitate to express her anger when the team has failed to secure a deal or when it has performed poorly, and they would also go out to drink and motivate one another to work harder. Her toughness eventually earned her the nicknames *onīsan* (older brother) and *bosu* (boss) among her subordinates, while her superiors began addressing her by name with the suffix -*kun* used mainly for male, as Umeda-*kun* or in the shortened form as Ume-*kun*.[8] To play along, Umeda would at times refer to herself using the male reference for the first person, as *ore* (the first person I).

Yet, Umeda knows that she is only perceived as having qualities similar to those of Japanese men, and will never be accepted as 'one of the boys.' She has never wished to be treated like a man either, but her colleagues have associated her behaviour as masculine only because she is perceived as lacking the typical feminine qualities. Umeda is flattered by this, interpreting others' response to her as affirming that she is not *futsū no onna* (an ordinary woman) who is weak, emotional, and incapable of doing demanding tasks that men are capable of doing. Yet, Umeda is conscious of the limits of her behaviour. To be likened to a male does not mean that she could do or say everything that Japanese men do. Her behaviour would invariably be judged based on that of a Japanese woman. Take drinking, for instance. Working women in Japan are able to legitimize drinking as an important extension of work, though it is still recognized as an important social activity for men, and the ability to consume large amount of alcohol symbolic of masculinity (Gotoh 1989: 953). Umeda's line of work involves frequent drinking, both among the workers and with clients. She could and does consume a copious amount of alcohol on a given evening, but she would never drink herself to a stupor. A man who cannot hold his drink may at times be criticized, but a drunken woman will be subject to more severe criticisms than an intoxicated *sararīman* lying unconscious on the street. Training her body to endure a large intake of alcohol without tipping over the edge is difficult, but necessary. With many of her subordinates eager to rise in the rank and take over her position at the helm, Umeda must always remain sober and composed so as not to be the object of relentless office gossips.

When she joined the job market after graduating from university, Umeda's first superior and mentor used to remind her that a job in sales and marketing is stressful, transitory, and competitive. Having been in sales for two decades, she knows that the team solidarity she has established and the loyalty she has worked hard to gain from her subordinates are superficial and short-lived. Sales targets are constantly being set and reset, while group performance is good only when targets are met or exceeded. Moreover, sales employees are ultimately concerned about their own individual performance and bonus. Since I first knew Umeda in the 2000s, I have often heard her lament about the weakening ties among employees, and feeling rather nostalgic about the kind of team loyalty that existed in the past. Yet, at the same time, she would not want these today, for the simple reason that the cherished values were by and intended for men as *senmonka* (experts or specialists), with women being *bugaisha* (outsiders) and *mongaikan* (amateurs) in sales, and also the corporate world.

It has been an arduous climb up the corporate ladder for Umeda to become a *senmonka*. The journey has demanded a tremendous amount of pain and sacrifice, as well as generated considerable stress and conflicts in her life. She has let go of several opportunities to marry in order to pursue a professional career, and sometimes regrets having made those decisions. Corporate working hours are long, but those for sales are much longer. Umeda is usually in the office by eight in the morning, and rarely reaches home before ten in the evening. She used to work every weekend in the past, and still works every Saturday. Though she is entitled to two weeks of annual leave, she hardly takes more than five days each year. When she developed various health problems due to years of sleep deprivation, irregular meals, heavy drinking, overwork, fatigue, and stress, Umeda took only annual leave to seek medical treatment. Claiming any medical leave would tarnish her employment records and increase her vulnerability for demotion and retrenchment. A spotless health record, however, might protect her job, and even improve her chances of getting one or more promotions.

As Umeda worries about how long she could preserve the façade of good health, the situation in the office suddenly changed after the arrival of Umeda's new boss. The new Senior Vice President of Strategy, Sales and Marketing was headhunted from a bigger and stronger rival company to re-organize and re-energize all sales operations. While Umeda has vied for the position herself, she knows that no woman would ever be promoted to that rank. She too knows that her new boss has plans to bring in new executives from his former workplace to replace some, if not all, the heads of sales divisions. Realizing that her days are numbered, Umeda willingly requested to be transferred to head the planning and product development division, so that she would move out of his reporting line, and hopefully get to remain in the company a little longer. It was approved instantly, after which several members of senior management praised her for having the foresight to 'step aside' while she is at the peak of her career, and not foolishly wait to be removed. As she explained to me:

> I have achieved what no woman has ever achieved in the company, and that is enough. I have played the game by other people's rules long and hard, and am very exhausted. I do not wish to fight any more or work any harder for an unattainable goal. I would be more emotionally drained and mentally troubled. The ceiling for me is so low that I could not climb any higher anyway. I have been in poor health and am unable to let anyone know about this. It is sad but this is the reality.
>
> By transferring out, I will not be perceived as stepping down, and so I could at least protect my pride and self-esteem. I have played the game well and it is time to acknowledge my time is up. A woman cannot act like a man simply because she is not one. I am, after all, only an imaginary *onīsan* who would be easily crushed by the huge army of *ojisan* (middle-aged and older men) up there in the company.
>
> (*laughs*)

From country girl, to dragon lady, pink monster, and master

While some women managers enact culturally constituted gender roles as a means of surviving in the corporate workplace, several appeal to other socially accepted, gender-related roles to cope with the various difficulties they encounter in their working life. For Ohno Rena, building a successful career in a large Japanese investment bank requires more than the power of the intellect, charm, and negotiation. She also has to tread skilfully on a tightrope with a good balance of subservience and domination, and carefully groom and manage her image to project her professional capabilities, business knowledge, and sophistication. Having graduated from a prestigious university in Japan, Ohno has an extensive network of alumni in the legal, finance, and banking industries, as well as large circles of friends and business contacts. The latest nickname given by her co-workers is *sensei* (teacher, or master), due to her fluency in several foreign languages; in-depth knowledge of current affairs and the global financial markets; appreciation of fine wines and international cuisines; and good taste in fashion. This is different from the previous nickname of *doragon redī* (dragon lady) coined by her co-workers who had construed Ohno's strict, disciplinarian, and 'no-nonsense' style of managing people and work as qualities of a ferocious, imposing woman. Ohno's latest nickname is also a stark contrast and positive change from much earlier ones that she had endured during the first few years in the bank when she was frequently referred to as *inaka mono* (country bumpkin), and *inaka musume* (country girl).

The change was due to the immense efforts made by Ohno to alter her image and be taken seriously by her co-workers and superiors. Ohno came from humble beginnings, who was born in a southern prefecture on Honshu island, and went to Tokyo to attend one of Japan's most prestigious universities. After entering the company, she was teased by for her 'strange' Japanese accent, lack of sophistication, and ignorance of many habits and practices in the country's capital city. Ohno has a strong interest in foreign languages since she was very young, and has taught herself Chinese, English, and Spanish. She had not been made to feel included during many social outings with her co-workers, Ohno decided to take evening classes to improve on her competency in these languages, one at a time, in order to overcome her feelings of alienation. While several co-workers had expressed discomfort and perhaps also envy on realizing Ohno's improved language competencies, she was relieved to have gained a superior's recognition which later earned her several overseas transfers.

Upon returning to Tokyo a few years later, Ohno was tasked with the management of the bank's division of institutional credit for overseas business. She was to gradually develop a 'tough management style' which she explained as necessary for supervising and managing difficult subordinates – particularly male employees – who took pride in their work as *ginkōman* (bankers) and were unwilling to submit to a female superior. Ohno was once again a newcomer, having been away from Tokyo for several years, and was, therefore, unfamiliar with the network of institutional clients whom her subordinates had established strong relations with. She had tried to develop good ties with both her subordinates and her employer's clients by going out drinking with them as often as she could, but she could not participate in some 'more serious bonding moments' among the men when they adjourned to late night entertainment places that cater mostly, and only, for male customers.

Perhaps it was out of desperation and frustration that led her to be firm and strict about her subordinates' entertainment activities and expenses. She soon learned she had been given nicknames such as *doragon redī, seitaigo*[9] (Empress of the Western Chamber in China), and *pinku monsuta*[10] (pink monster). Complaints about her also spread, till she became known as a demanding and domineering woman towards her subordinates, and was unsupportive of their career advancement. Following several poor performance reviews, Ohno began heeding her superior's advice to soften her management style in order to reduce or alleviate the conflicts and confrontations she had with her subordinates.

> My boss said that my job was at risk, and that neither my language competencies nor knowledge about the bank's overseas business would save

> me if I did not try hard enough to win my subordinates' support and respect. It was very discouraging. When a Japanese man is tough on his subordinates, he is respected for being a good, efficient leader. When a woman is tough, she is given derogatory names...

Once again, Ohno turned to self-learning, though this time it was to improve on her knowledge about international cuisines, expensive alcoholic beverages, and all that was important to know about cosmopolitan lifestyle that would enhance her image and position her as a legitimate figure in the upper rung of Japan's business world. She would spend her weekends visiting *sakaguras* (sake breweries); attending wine-tasting classes; sampling a wide variety of alcoholic beverages; and dining with friends to try out cuisines of different countries. Ohno would also use her annual leave to visit vineyards outside Japan, and had even spent weeks to learn cooking in France, Israel, Italy, and Spain. Watching television programmes on food and drinks became an everyday routine, while her collection of books, magazines, and DVDs also grew. Ohno made sure to share her expanded knowledge – acquired at her own expense – with co-workers while they were out drinking after work, partly to impress them, and also to help them impress clients. Over time, she gradually became known as *sensei*.

Ohno would often laugh at her own naivete in trying to find a 'miracle' that would salvage her career in banking. More importantly, she could not disappoint her father who had worked very hard since her mother's death to raise and educate three children by himself. Ohno's oldest brother is a civil engineer in a large corporation in Fukuoka, while her second brother manages the logistics operations of a medium-sized company in Osaka. While Ohno's father is proud that all his three children have become *sararīman*, the former accounts clerk is most delighted that his only daughter is a *ginkōman*. As the old man had repeatedly told Ohno, the status of a banker may not be as prestigious as that of a lawyer or a doctor, but a *ginkōman* commands more respect than an ordinary *sararīman*, and a *toshi ginkōka* (investment banker) is simply *kurēmu do ra kurēmu* (crème de la crème) among *ginkōman*. But what her father does not, and probably would never, know is how difficult the job has been for Ohno, or that there are so many limitations and obstacles that she would have to experience because she is a *ginkō ūman* (woman banker), and not a *ginkōman*.

Even after she had gradually gained her subordinates' respect as *sensei* for being knowledgeable about their line of work and also as a good mentor, Ohno could not develop strong relations with clients or participate in important business negotiations in entertainment places such as a hostess club, strip bar, or golf course as the male employees could. She had once joined a few subordinates and business clients on a golf trip to a resort, where she had spent the evenings by herself, while the men took a dip in a hot spring together, went for a massage, and then proceeded to enjoying voyeuristic entertainment that is catered exclusively for male pleasure.

The only space for this *ginkō ūman* to strategize is that of after-work drinking with her co-workers where she could try to manage their attitude towards her, in order to minimize any conflict that might arise in the workplace, and allow her to protect her job.

The task of managing becomes increasingly difficult in today's flexible work environment, where relations between employees are transitory, competitive, disharmonious, and unstable. After-work drinking may be a necessary means for managers to stabilize and improve relations with co-workers and protect their job, but it is done at the expense of their own time and money. It is also emotionally demanding and physically exhausting. While the women's struggles are also shared by male managers, the former are to deal with additional difficulties relating to their gender. As the aforementioned narratives elucidate, enacting culturally constituted gender and other socially accepted roles may for some women managers be useful coping strategies, but these are transitory and unstable means of managing with immediate or short-term situations, with little or no promise of alleviating the varying challenges that many female corporate executives experience in the workplace. But, at the same time, not all women in supervisory and managerial positions could utilize such strategies in the office, and are to find various other means of coping with the difficulties they encounter.

To make matters worse, their precarious position as managers has also been exacerbated by some innovative corporate practices that have emerged in recent years. Among the most prevalent and particularly problematic practices is that of nominal management or empty promotion, that is, the elevation of employees to supervisory and managerial positions which increases their workload but not necessarily their salary or authority, as the next chapter will elucidate in greater detail.

Notes

1 This combines the Japanese word *nomu* (to drink) with part of the English word 'communication.' The word *nomunikēshon* became widely used recently to portray drinking as a way of facilitating communication.

2 The word *ofisu* is a romanization of the English word 'office.'

3 This refers to the fashion doll Barbie that was created and marketed by the American toy company Mattel Inc. in 1959. The popularity of Barbie has spawned successful global industries of related merchandise such as accessories and clothes, but it has also been subject of criticisms, controversies, and lawsuits, for typecasting women as sexy objects.

4 A White Paper introduced by the Ministry of Health, Labour and Welfare in 2012 to curb corporate bullying and power harassment is to be enforced as a new legislation in 2020. See more details and discussions in Chapter 5.

5 Given that the nature of a sales job involves a lot of drinking and entertaining, there is considerable pressure on Japanese men working in sales to live up to the image of *eigyōman* as charismatic, talkative, tough, and strong drinkers.

6 Many employers are exploiting a loophole in Japan's antiquated labour laws, which states that employees who become supervisors and managers are not protected by a maximum limit 40 working hours a week, nor are they entitled to

receive payment for overtime worked (Ouchi 2010). This will be discussed in greater detail in Chapter 4.

7 Based on the English word 'service,' the Japanese word *sābisu* is used to describe a service as requiring no payment. The term *sābisu zangyō* thus means overtime work with no remuneration.

8 The suffix-*kun* is usually attached to a man's first name when one addresses a friend or a family member. While the suffix-*chan* is used for both men and women in a casual context, the suffix-*kun* is hardly used to address a woman. In most formal situations, the suffix-*san* is attached to the family name of both men and women.

9 This title was that of Empress Dowager Cixi (1835–1908) who ruled China for 47 years as regent to Emperor Tongzhi (1856–1875) and Emperor Guangxu (1871–1908) during the Qing dynasty from 1861 till her death in 1908. See discussions on Japanese media representations of women as *seitaigo* in Chapter 2.

10 *Pinku monsuta* is a romanization of the English words pink monster. The colour pink is generally associated with women, as the term 'pink-collar' work is used to refer to jobs that women typically do.

4 In the office

As nominal managers and corporate props

Legal loophole and the rise of nominal management

'What does it mean to be a manager?' This question is frequently asked by most of my informants whose mixed experiences lead them to develop variegated views of their positions in the workplace, the importance of their roles, and their sense of self-worth as professionally qualified, competent, and capable individuals. Despite having been given opportunities to enter the historically male domain of salaried work, Japanese women persistently encounter difficulties pertaining to their being female. And despite having been taught to embrace the importance of having individual aspirations and shouldering *jikosekinin* (self-responsibility) to achieve *jibunrashī seikatsu* (lifestyle of one's choice) and *jūjitsukan* (self-fulfilment) (Cave 2001: 177; Ho 2018: 31), many female corporate executives have come to realize that the prevailing merit-based, performance-oriented work environment is too limited and mired in contradictions to help them make meaningful sense of being promoted to managerial positions and performing their roles as corporate managers. A sleuth of neoliberal discourses in modern business on 'self-management' and the 'enterprising self' may have become pervasive in Japan with the rise of managerialism in recent decades, but wide chasms exist between rhetoric and reality that they introduce conflicts and ambivalence in the lives of many corporate managers, male and female (Gagné 2018: 75). The use of managerialism as an ideological tool to incentivize corporate managers and transform their perceptions of responsibilities has been an integral part of neoliberal change in post-bubble Japan, as it allows the state and corporations to roll back on their roles as welfare providers (Dore 2000: 11).

Managerialism in modern business which promotes responsibility and efficiency blends well in the neoliberal environment of flexible labour, where the importance of freedom and individualism is given a strong emphasis by the rhetoric of entrepreneurialism (Chauvière and Mick 2011: 137). Together, they form a powerful ideology for organizations to engineer goals and create an oppressive regime to serve those goals (Klikauer 2015: 1106). Since the rise of managerialism in the US in the 1960s, the ideological power of the business practice has remained in the disjuncture between the rhetoric of modern management methods and the reality of their implementation (Chauvière and Mick 2011: 137). Corporate managers are often ideologically pushed by the so-called sophisticated human resource approaches to pursue professional competence, individual initiative, personal development, leadership grooming, self-responsibility, and high performance. Yet, in reality, managerialism utilizes a 'grab bag of managerial tools' that demand managers to constantly perform a wide array of functions with unattainable targets, such as budget reporting, conducting of statistical evaluations of tasks, calculating of efficiency, measuring of productivity, and benchmarking of work performance against ideal standards of excellence. At the same time, income stability and job security are increasingly being eroded by the neoliberal environment of flexible work where corporate activities are underpinned by cost management and headcount control. Criticisms of the varied practices of managerialism have proliferated since the beginning of 1990s, including the dissenting voices of intellectuals such as Pierre Bourdieu, Michel de Certeau, Vincent de Gaulejac, Alain Erhenberg, Michel Foucault, Jürgen Habermas, Henri Lefebve, and Jean-Pierre Le Goff (Ibid.). The common interpretations of the impact of managerialism are that the formalized systems of managing, reporting, and evaluating actually disable employees from doing their job; disconnect workers from themselves as individuals for confusing organizational goals as their own; produce angst and anxiety in the workplace; and have long-term implementations on the mental and emotional states of managers (De Gaulejac 2009, 2011; Ehrenberg 1991; Le Goff 1996).

The practice of managerialism in Japan shares similarities with that in Europe and North America, though it also encompasses a variety of sociocultural values that are linked closely to local political and economic agendas. The adoption of Western forms of managerialism began in Japan during the bubble era in the 1980s under the leadership of former Prime Minister Nakasone Yasuhiro (1982–1987). They later grew in popularity with active promulgations of neoliberal reforms implemented by subsequent prime ministers, especially Hashimoto Ryutaro (1996–1998) and Obuchi Keizo (1998–2000) after the demise of the country's bubble economy (Tiberghien 2014: 27). Following in the footsteps of his predecessor and mentor Koizumi Junichiro (2000–2006), the current Prime Minister Shinzo Abe launched a set of fiscal and labour reforms – known as 'Abenomics' – in 2013 to intensify the neoliberalization of labour and the economy which sparked considerable debates and contentions (Gagné 2018: 67–8). Abe's neoliberal reforms have been more rhetorical than real, in that his various policies on deregulation and labour actually empower corporations and disempower workers, albeit in the name of promoting greater individual freedom, choice, and autonomy (Suzuki 2015: 168).

The rise of managerialism in Japan marked a radical shift from the postwar practice of 'companyism,' to the neoliberal deployment of 'individualism' in post-bubble era. Postwar political and economic reforms had relegated the burden of providing stability, security, and social welfare from the state to corporations (Borovoy 2011: 62). Ronald Dore (1973: 370–1) explains this as a shift from the prewar system of 'welfare statism' to the postwar system of 'welfare corporatism.' This marked the retreat of the state from its role as the main welfare provider. It also pointed to the importance of companies as the primary domains of identity-production and formation of affiliations for workers, who, in turn, were to pledge their loyalty and commitment (Olcott 2010: 26–7).

As companies struggled to raise productivity and profitability following the demise of Japan's bubble economy in the early 1990s, the state turned to deploying neoliberal strategies by introducing individuality in educational reforms, and promoting flexible employment, along with managerialism and entrepreneurialism (Moriya 2005; Nomura 2000; Tatsumichi and Morishima 2004). In transforming 'Old Japan' into 'New Japan' that seeks to align itself more closely with major global economies, the neoliberal reforms in Japan invariably also shifted the structure of the workforce from a rigid, bureaucratic, and inefficient 'company-centred' system, into an 'individual-centred,' performance-based merit system. The new system was – and still is – 'promoted as democratic, progressive and empowering for individual employees' (Gagné 2018: 73), since company employees and managers were making sacrifices for their own personal gains and not those of the company. Workers would also be motivated to work harder, and to invest heavily in improving their professional capabilities at their own expense, which would eventually reap benefits for their employers (Gagné 2019: 13).

While managerialism becomes a powerful and economical strategy for companies in meeting their primary objectives of raising staff productivity and profitability, a loophole in Japan's antiquated labour law permitted employers to turn the practice into a formidable tool of exploitation to save on staff costs through the pervasive use of a practice known as *nabakari kanrishoku* (quasi or nominal management) (Ouchi 2008; Yashiro 2002). Technically, a promotion to the position of 'manager' ought to be accompanied by an increase in salary and staff benefits to compensate for the additional responsibilities an employee is expected to undertake, and also by an enhancement of the worker's authority and more active participation in corporate decision-making. This does not appear to be the case in many companies, where promotions come with additional workload, but minimal change in remuneration, benefits, or authority (Ogura 2010; Ouchi 2008; Takahashi 2005; Yashiro 2002). In some cases, newly promoted managers might actually experience a reduction in their gross salaries in real terms, due to the loss of entitlement to overtime remuneration that is stipulated by Japan's outmoded labour laws (Ho 2018: 37).

According to Item (ii) Article 41 of Japan's Labor Standards Act (1947), employees who are *kantokusha* (supervisors) and *kanrisha* (managers) are 'persons in positions of supervision or management,' or 'persons handling confidential matters regardless of the types of enterprise.'[1] As such, they are not protected by a maximum limit to the number of working hours, and employers are not required by law to pay employees for overtime worked. To be sure, not all corporations in Japan avoid paying their managers overtime compensation. Many in fact do, and could freely determine whether or not to do so, and also to set the overtime rates. Employers are thus able to reduce staff costs by creating managerial positions and promoting employees, as well as raise profitability by exploiting workers' fear of being made redundant, and the ambitions of others to rise in the ranks.

It is difficult to ascertain the ubiquity of this cosmetic arrangement of nominal management, though the increasing number of reported cases gradually drew the attention of the authorities and the media in Japan (Ogura 2010; Ouchi 2008; Yashiro 2002). The Japan Institute for Labor Policy and Training (henceforth JILPT), the research arm of the country's Ministry of Health, Labour and Welfare, published a number of reports in the late 2000s on the prevalence of nominal management. A report written by Ouchi Shinya (2010: 72) attributed the rising incidence of nominal management to the 'defectiveness' of this legislation, and called for it to be revised in order to prevent employers from utilizing nominal management as an 'attractive' means of controlling labour costs to exploit workers. He argues that the terms 'supervisors' and 'managers' have 'no clear definition under law' other than the vague description as 'persons in the organizational structure who are in positions of responsibility,' that companies could easily construe low-level section managers as such persons 'in positions of responsibility' that many managers are promoted 'in title alone' but 'go about their normal duties' with unspecified working hours and no entitlement of overtime remuneration (Ibid.: 74). Ouchi also highlighted a bias in court rulings of reported cases of nominal management that favoured employers, and called for the state to closely examine the 'details of the person's job duties, his/her responsibilities and authority, and the actual working terms' when cases have been reported (Ibid.). He cited several court rulings that had ordered employers to pay out minimal compensation to employees because the employers were 'not the only ones at fault,' and that employees were also to be blamed for their 'willingness' to become 'managers' (Ibid.: 77).

Indeed, many employees are willing to become managers, since getting a promotion is supposed to signify an obvious progression of their receiving recognition for having performed well at work, and being rewarded by an opportunity to take on more responsibilities with a higher salary. In post-bubble Japan when permanent employment is becoming rarer and the risk of *tenshoku* (job-changing) higher, employees would readily welcome what seems like a career advancement as it is perceived to promise greater job security. Yet, the fact that the labour laws of the country should be designed, or are yet to be re-designed to keep up with the broader work environment, in such a way that employees are actually to blame for accepting promotions invariably creates what Jean-Pierre Le Goff (1996) describes as a 'disjuncture' between reality and rhetoric to generate experiences of angst, anxiety, frustrations, and disillusionment among managers.

Official statistics are still unavailable on the prevalence of nominal management in reality. JILPT has also not released any updated study on the situation since the late 2000s. While the prevalence of nominal management obviously affects all white-collar workers, both male and female, women's willingness to accept lower pay than their male counterparts and their marginal position in the workplace vis-à-vis that male employees render them particularly vulnerable to exploitation by employers. Moreover, with Abe's rhetorical push for womenomics, promoting women to supervisory and managerial positions – albeit nominally – also enables employers to strategically project a semblance of conformity and enhance their corporate image at relatively low cost.

Based on my field data, nearly two-thirds of the 160 corporate managers – and also 40 male – whom I interviewed in cities across Japan since 2002 disclosed that they had at least one experience of promotion with a real salary decrease. More than 80 per cent of my informants said that they had their pay increase delayed – from two to 15 months – due to a variety of issues, especially their employer's budget limitations or cashflow difficulties. Nearly all female managers had their ascent to higher levels of management delayed due to corporate restructuring that increased the number of middle-management positions they had to fill before they could be promoted further. None of the male managers were aware of such a change in the organizational structure in their workplace, and were hence unable to respond. Half of the 140 women managers I interviewed had experienced one or more demotions in their managerial title, which were also attributed to necessary restructuring of their employer's business operations.

From a survey that I conducted of 30 companies over the same period, I learned that nearly all had changed their organizational structure to improve on their corporate profile by multiplying the number of both managerial positions and female employees, while at the same time also placing more women in newly created positions of management. One retail company, for example, once had two managerial positions in each of its 15 divisions in 1995 when the company had a total of 500 employees. Today, the headcount had increased to 700 employees who work in 20 divisions, each of which is headed by five managers. The retail company's management team has more than tripled from 30 managers in 1995, to 100 today. Furthermore, the human resource director said that 60 of all the managerial positions are occupied by women, which he attributed to an initiative to significantly enhance the company's image and profile for shareholders, investors, and the general public of its commitment to promote greater gender equality.

Yet, upon closer scrutiny, the organizational chart shows that only one-third of the female managers in the company are full-time employees, and only one female occupies the highest management position of the 20 divisions. Moreover, there is no female in the company's board of directors.

From an interview with the managing director of another company, I gathered that while the financial services provider too has expanded its female management workforce following a threefold increase in managerial positions since the late 1990s, two-thirds of the women managers are temporary and part-time employees. This company, like most others in my study and perhaps most companies in Japan,[2] also has no female participation in the highest management tier or as member of the board of directors. While there are variations across companies, they share similar patterns of making changes to managerial titles, creating new positions, adding new management layers, and promoting of both regular and irregular employees.

Granted, the sample is too small to be representative of the real experiences of all corporate managers in Japan, and the data could hardly be used to gauge the prevalence of nominal management. Nonetheless, it provides a general sense of some corporate practices and experiences of corporate managers to shed some light on how employers could take advantage of the current work environment to utilize nominal management as a convenient and also powerful tool to further their goals. Employers have in their favour more than a loophole in Japan's antiquated labour laws and the government's promotion of womenomics. The changing demographics in post-bubble Japan have also contributed much to strengthening employers' ability to manipulate the situation. First, the flexible work environment has provided opportunities for an increasing number of women who had quit working to get married or to give birth, but later returned to the job market after their divorce.

This is one of the reasons for the M-shaped curve of Japan's female workforce participation, which typically shows a dip in the number of working women aged 30–35 years, and an increase again among those aged 35–45 years (SHJ 2018: 124). The divorce rates in Japan have historically been on the increase, from 1.51 per 1,000 of the population in 1983, to 2.03 in 2006, and later to 1.7 in 2017 (Ibid.: 19). For many of my informants, especially those who are divorced single mothers, having a steady job is necessary for meeting their household expenses, and a promotion – even if it is a mere change in job title – is more crucial to maintaining or improving their chances of securing the next job with a reasonably decent salary. Kazuya Ogura (2010: 69) describes this as the vicious circle of 'playing managers' which perpetuates the problem of long working hours without overtime payment.

Despite being aware of its long-term implications, many women managers feel trapped in this vicious circle of allowing themselves to work as nominal managers to enhance their resume in the hope of getting a new job that offers similar or better terms of employment, but realizing that the title of the next job could also be a cosmetic one that comes with similar or worse terms. Since women typically occupy low- to mid-level managerial positions, and given also that middle-aged and older women face greater difficulty in advancing their career, acquiescing to a cosmetic arrangement is also necessary for some of these women managers to keep their job for as long as they could. The fact that their fears and dilemmas are evident to employers makes them particularly susceptible to exploitation. The multifarious ways in which employers adopt managerialism and nominal management to keep up with the changing business conditions in post-bubble Japan compound the impact that negative media portrayals of women with professional careers in Japan and the performing of culturally constituted gender roles expectations have on many women managers' self-esteem and their relations with co-workers. They also have far more serious ramifications on the sustainability of their economic life and sense of self-worth, as the following narratives will illustrate. Some women wonder about what it means to be a corporate manager, while others mull over the meaninglessness of being one. Their common experiences of confusion and frustrations exacerbate their feelings of fear and insecurity, with long-term implications on their emotional, mental, and physical health which might pervade their personal and family lives.

Corporate managers in name

Imitating a manager

Arai Ayumi was 29 years old when she was promoted to Team Leader of the legal division of a publicly listed game software development company. Since my work in Tokyo then required frequent discussions and negotiations with several of her team members and other colleagues, I had the opportunity to watch her interact with co-workers. I was curious to note how progressive the company was to have women heading several divisions. Besides the legal team, several other divisions such as Finance, Treasury, Administration, Corporate Communications, and Marketing teams were each headed by a woman. However, like Arai, each team leader reported to a male Senior Team Leader, and all higher ranked executives were male. It had puzzled as to why Arai would at times not only perform the tasks assigned to her subordinates – three male and one female – and still give them credit, but why she would also show willingness to run errands for them as though she was their subordinate. It was not until a year later after I returned to Tokyo as a graduate student that we had a long conversation about her behaviour in the office.

After the company was bought over by another Japanese firm, a new organizational structure was established to give the combined entity a modern image similar to high-technology companies in Silicon Valley. Many job titles were renamed. The word 'team' was used instead of 'section' and 'department,' while 'leader' replaced 'supervisor' and 'section chief.' More importantly, the company also changed many low-level job titles by adding the word 'leader' – for example, from 'Legal Assistant' to 'Junior Team leader' – which was said to incentivize employees and raise their productivity.

The most radical move was to have as many female team leaders as possible, except for the Sales, Technical Support, and Product Development divisions. However, this change had little to do with improving gender inequality in the workplace. Arai laughed and explained that it was to save the company on the expense of having a secretary or assistant in each department by having the female team leader perform all administrative and secretarial functions. Arai describes her job as that of *manējā no mane* (imitating a manager) performing the varied tasks of a supervisor, subordinate, tea lady, secretary, and also servant.

A 'floating' manager

Until today, Ishida Izumi and her former colleagues still continue to talk with disbelief and bewilderment about the biggest staff meeting they have ever attended while they were working for one of Japan's largest media and telecommunications companies. Her employer had been on a buying spree for several years, snapping up 'good deals' across Japan and all over the world, that the words restructuring and job redundancy were constantly buzzing in the office. Everyone was waiting in anxious anticipation and unease about whether they would be the next batch to be fired. Then an announcement came that a staff meeting was to be held in a convention hall where all the top corporate executives would be present. Ishida was in her mid-thirties back then, and thought that her position as assistant manager in one of the many sales and marketing divisions might be removed like many jobs in the company.

The divorced single mother dreaded the prospect of having to do *tenshoku* all over again, having spent several years after her divorce moving from one part-time job to another until she was finally given her first opportunity to settle in what she had thought was a regular job.

The announcement made at the staff meeting was to later leave Ishida surprised and perplexed. To increase efficiency and accelerate the approval process, the company would trim the size of all divisions to teams comprising no more than 10–15 employees who would report directly to their own team leader. A Supra Team Leader would act as the Chief Executive Officer (CEO) of several teams, with the assistance of a floating committee of mentors and consultants who would oversee the work of a few Supra Team Leaders. Most significantly, no team member would have the same title, as each would be given a job title to highlight a unique area of specialization. Team members would also be 'available for hire' by other teams should their assistance and service be required, and this was highly encouraged to raise a team's profits and minimize its operating costs. There were too many changes for Ishida to remember, as she had crammed into her head more than it had the capacity to retain.

What mattered to her the most was that she and many co-workers had been demoted in principle in exchange for a fancier job title and additional workload. She was previously one step away from the position of Manager, but was now five positions removed from that of Team Leader. She had not been given a new or revised contract of employment, which left her feeling confused about whether she would now be entitled to a little overtime pay or more benefits. All queries relating to this were dismissed as having low priority compared to the more pressing tasks of implementing the new organizational structure, and also to the lack of clarity as to who would be responsible for dealing with such a matter. After seeing the retrenchment of many co-workers, Ishida became afraid to lose her own job and decided to not pursue what her Team Leader referred to as 'a trivial matter.'

She is still working for the company today, though she has been 'hired' by so many teams that she no longer considers herself as belonging to any. Ishida likens herself to a *yakatabune* (boathouse) which floats from place to place with no specific destination or purpose, other than serving the interest and needs of her employer. She still retains her rather vague job title of Special Project Team Manager which has remained unchanged for the past 11 years. When asked about her experience in the company, Ishida responded like this:

> I do not know what to say because I really do not know what I am doing. I manage unimportant tasks, not projects. I do menial administrative work and anything that I have been instructed to do. I am so exhausted, confused and demoralized that I do not have any confidence to manage even if I was given a real manager's job to do. I am just living from day to day, and trying to be optimistic about not getting fired. If this is the kind of work that some company managers do, then perhaps I should be thankful…

Lost in a forbidden forest

Unlike Ishida, Endo Eriko is often angry with herself for having allowed herself to be 'cheated' by her former employer. However, she shares Ishida's experience of having her career advancement delayed by repeated rounds of corporate restructuring by the advertising company where she worked for eight years. She was the object of envy for being the first among her peers to lead a team after joining the agency for only two years. Aged 28 years back then, Endo was also the youngest Team Leader, and was managing the largest team of nine members of consultants. She had felt elated and proud to note the 'bold' and 'progressive' move by a 'traditional Japanese company' in replacing old-fashioned job titles – such as *shunin* (supervisor), *kakarichō* (deputy head of a section or division), *kachō* (head of a section or division), and *buchō* (head of a department) – with contemporary, American-styled ones such as Team Leader, Vice President, Senior Vice President, and Executive Vice President. Her active participation in business planning and increased autonomy in executing business initiatives motivated Endo to work harder. She would typically clock no less 80 hours of work in a given week. She would also top the annual performance charts, which had earned her an award for being the most promising contender for the position of Vice President. But her hopes were soon dashed by a subsequent restructuring which added two new positions above hers. She would have to first be Senior Team Leader and then Executive Team Leader before she could be considered for Vice President. Endo said that the restructuring had put her career progression back by four years.

Her desired goal became more elusive with another reorganization a year later. This time, two further positions were introduced below that of Vice President: Teams Strategic Director and Deputy Vice President. And that was not all. The latest move also reduced the size of each team, and split the responsibilities of every managerial position reporting to the Vice President. Though this company justified the changes on the grounds that they would lighten each manager's workload and enhance the productivity of each team, Endo and her co-workers saw the changes as having diminished the authority of each managerial position to the handling of mundane tasks. This made them more dispensable. As she explained:

> Each team was like a class and the team leader its representative. Anyone could be asked to do the job. We were only class representatives, not managers. In fact, the so-called flat corporate structure turned most of us into foot soldiers who were further removed from the real centre of power up there somewhere.

Endo described her experience like being in a *meiro* (maze), and her hopes of ever getting the desired promotion a *genzo* (illusion). For her, being a manager in the company was like someone who has entered the small, forbidden forest known *Yawata no Yabushirazu* (Yawata's Mystery) in Chiba prefecture from where one could never get out. Endo began contemplating a job change, but was worried that she might have to start all over again from the bottom in a new workplace. Perhaps she could stay. After all, she was not particularly displeased with the salary increments following each promotion. Her annual bonuses were also fairly computed based on the value of new businesses that a manager had generated, and Endo was always among the top five in the agency. She would have stayed longer had her employer not announced yet another restructuring. A further layering of the middle management would mean another few years' wait for a promotion to Vice President. She was already burnt out, and had lost all faith in the company. After she mustered enough courage to resign, Endo was unemployed for nearly two years before she took up employment as Senior Vice President in a bigger American firm. She had this to say during a conversation over coffee in July 2019:

> Companies in Japan are creating fancy job titles like items on a menu for cosmetic surgery that are only for improving on their image. These

> nice titles make companies look good, but they make workers feel empty and insecure because their positions are meaningless and temporary. We are just makeup, which makes you look good while it is there, but it is readily removable.

Endo's experiences highlight the challenges generated by the rise of managerialism which, together with the practice of nominal management, heighten employees' feelings of anxiety, frustrations, and sense of futility in their career pursuits. Though nominal management is clearly a useful strategy and powerful ideological tool for employers to reconfigure their existing resources for greater management control and efficient operation in ways that yield little benefit for employees, it is difficult to define or be proven in any litigation. This is because managerialism under the neoliberal work regime of today is a legitimate corporate tool that is widely recognized as an integral part of smart business practice. As Max Weber (1958: 182) once remarked, capitalistic practices often utilize extreme forms of instrumental reasoning to shape workers into becoming '[S]pecialists without spirit, sensualities without heart.' Managerialism is one such extreme form of rational instrument in today's neoliberalized capitalistic system, in which being managers requires individuals to internalize specific values that encompass the management of their identity and emotions – namely hopes, fears, and expectations of success – in manners that require them to train and discipline themselves into becoming flexible and adaptable, proclaimed in the name of self-empowerment and self-actualization. This form of managerialism under neoliberal capitalism is said to have mutated into managerial capitalism (Klikauer 2015: 1105). This is a new disciplinary form of governmental rationality (Foucault 1991), and a pervasive political project that drives individuals to disciplining themselves willingly as they govern the self by internalizing the values of efficiency, productivity, and performance results in alignment with the goals of organizations (Klikauer 2015: 1105).

This accounts for why, despite their experience of increased susceptibility and vulnerability, corporate managers are often at odds with themselves for desiring the recognition and rewards from the very same system that also exploits and abuses those desires that it encourages individuals to embrace. The stronger individuals' aspirations for career advancement are, the more they internalize the need for self-regulation by obsessing over self-improvements such as pursuing professional qualifications to help them *kyaria appu* (career up), as they say in Japan, and hence the more they are to assume full responsibility for their own action and taking the blame for poor work performance. In doing so, they are reinforcing the vicious circle of legitimizing the abusive potential of the practice of managerialism that offers little or no assurance of positive gains, and intensifying their feelings and experiences of anxiety, frustrations, and precarity. As a pseudo arrangement of managerialism, nominal management aggravates this situation as it flourishes in the absence of an official mechanism to properly monitor and regulate corporate abuse.

Victims of an arbitrary appraisal system

One problematic practice of managerialism that has come to feature prominently in the neoliberal corporate workplace in Japan today is the use of feedback or peer reviews as a key mode of assessing one's job performance. In addition to dealing with the problems of high staff turnover and nominal management, managers' jobs are at risk as their performance is increasingly subject to evaluations by junior employees, some of whom may seek to express their grievances or vent their frustrations about their work conditions. Women executives are particularly vulnerable, not only because their value decreases and expendability increases with age, but that they have to often deal with junior employees who do not take well to being given orders by a female superior, especially when she is young, a part-time or temporary manager. Their ability to command respect and authority would deteriorate further if it is common knowledge in an office that certain managerial positions are nominal and not real. To have their work performance appraised under such conditions could generate conflicts among workers, and even pose serious threats to their job that might cause some managers to be denied of a promotion, be demoted, or even dismissed.

Fire everywhere

Among the many difficulties that Nukaga Nao has had to face was that of being sandwiched between her superiors and subordinates as a nominal manager at her former workplace. On the one hand, she had to perform tasks according to verbal instructions from her superiors and compile written records that complied with company policies and regulatory bodies. On the other hand, she had to present instructions to her subordinates as though they came from her, and hence she had to bear all responsibilities for her division's action. The fact that Nukaga's job performance was evaluated at both ends on such a tenuous basis gave her many sleepless nights and untold stress that she eventually resigned after three years on the job.

Her position was that of Senior Manager in the Compliance and Risk Management division of a large Japanese manufacturer of food and beverages. She had five subordinates, and reported to a member of the company's board of directors. Nukaga was appointed to the position following a transfer from human resource department where she worked for 11 years. The company was preparing ahead of the new legislation on curbing workplace bullying and power harassment, and demonstrate to external auditors and the local authorities that it had taken adequate measures to prevent, monitor, and resolve a diversity of cases. More importantly, the company was also vying to be named as a 'women friendly employer' under Prime Minster Abe's initiatives on womenomics. Nukaga was thus promoted along with some 12 other female co-workers to each fill a more senior managerial position within the company. She was told that it would be a huge leap in her career development, since the compliance division would have a direct reporting line to the highest level of management within the company, and its activities would have a significant impact of the company's public image and reputation in the future.

Nukaga had not anticipated what was to come. She could only remember then how thrilled she had felt and readily accepted the transfer and promotion, even though the salary increment was minimal. There would be a considerable amount of new things to learn, and compliance work would be more interesting than her old job as Payroll Manager. Several weeks after joining the new division, Nukaga realized that her position as senior manager and those of her female peers were not the only cosmetic arrangement the company had made. She was initially excited about working with her team in compiling a new list of appropriate and inappropriate behaviours for a revised staff manual. She was also enthusiastic about the regular reports submitted to the board of directors and internal auditors which contained an exhaustive checklist and quantitative analyses of all cases of complaints, disputes, and rule violations, as well as the percentage of cases resolved. The biggest comfort was her team's ability to resolve many of the complaints about abusive employees, bad behaviour, and malpractices within the company. For a short period of time, Nukaga had thought her new job to be meaningful and important, which somehow offered relief to the stress, pressure, and exhaustion from long hours of work.

Then one day, Nukaga began receiving verbal instructions from her superior to follow up only on specific types of complaints, and to ignore all others. The items were to change periodically, subject to 'quotas' decided by the board of directors for each type of complaints. The aim was to not only show that the company was doing a thorough job in monitoring, preventing, and resolving a diversity of cases, but to also manage the company's public image by controlling the amount of reported cases of inappropriate behaviour, workplace abuse, disputes among employees and rule violations. When the number of complaints about sexual harassment, for example, was unexpectedly high over a certain period of time, Nukaga's team was instructed to manage the level of this type of complaint by dismissing new cases and not officially record them. When the level fell too low, Nukaga's team could perhaps re-open dismissed cases. Moreover, given the ultimate goal was to achieve a high rate of success, Nukaga's team must thus bear the responsibility of investigating reported cases that could be resolved, or risk putting their job on the line.

The hardest part of Nukaga's job at that time was her inability to explain to her subordinates why she was selective about the cases reported to her office, which placed her job at risk. Her performance was eventually to be evaluated poorly by her subordinates, who had thought Nukaga biased and negligent in overlooking too many important complaints. This thus reinforced her subordinates' perception of Nukaga as incompetent and incapable of doing her job well as head of compliance. They had not regarded Nukaga favourably to begin with. Her promotion was widely known within the company to be a cosmetic arrangement to beautify the company's profile by promoting more women to managerial positions. It was difficult for Nukaga to explain that she was not responsible for being selective in accepting complaints. It would be embarrassing to be perceived as a senior manager who was powerless, hence reinforcing her subordinates' view that she was a mere puppet. She would also risk exposing the company for violating regulations. Much as she had tried to gently hint to her subordinates while they were drinking after work, Nukaga could not convince them to believe that the senior management would set such quotas. To command respect and understanding from her subordinates was challenging, especially from three part-time employees who would not hesitate to be candid in evaluating their leader, since they would not work long enough for the company should they need to be questioned about their appraisals of Nukaga.

At the same time, Nukaga had also been appraised poorly by her superiors for failing to follow their instructions closely by reporting too many complaints on particular types of practices which were considered to be undesirable. She was reminded by her boss of the 'special treatment' by the board of directors in promoting her, and warned to not lose their trust by not doing as she was instructed. Caught between the frying pan and the fire, Nukaga had felt her position as a nominal manager to be like that of a lone firefighter who was helpless, vulnerable, and trapped. As she explained to me:

> I was already very disappointed with the board's demand to maintain quotas on complaints, and their lack of sincerity in dealing with many problems within the company. I had no voice. I could not explain this to my subordinates, who misunderstood me and blamed me for not managing the team properly. The compliance department was not set up to comply with the laws and regulations in Japan, but to comply with the wishes of the company's board of directors. It was a meaningless job… an impossible one too. Everywhere I turned there was fire. And I was always alone in fighting the fire…

Nukaga was soon burned out by the mounting level of stress and frustrations that she had experienced, and resigned. The 48-year-old has returned to her old line of work in human resource, and is much happier working as Assistant Payroll Manager in a small Japanese trading company. She is today still troubled by the countless cases that were dismissed, and often thinks about how unfair it had been for those co-workers who had been victims of abusive behaviour in her former workplace. Her other concern is about reconciling herself with the reality of being a nominal manager, and having to deal with the anxiety and frustrations of being one. Another woman who has similar concerns is Kojima Kaeko.

Permanent flower in the workplace for display

Kojima is currently unemployed, and has been in therapy for two years to help her recover from depression and regain her self-confidence. The eight years she had spent at her former workplace had depleted her energy, drained her confidence, and nearly destroyed her life, as she explained to me one day. She remembered how dispirited she was when she spent two years going from interview to interview with no job offer prior to joining her former workplace. Kojima was more than relieved to be eventually hired as Senior Marketing Manager by a Japanese-European joint venture company, which had promised her a promotion to Marketing Director within two years. However, she worked there for eight years not as Senior Marketing Manager, but Senior Manager of Human Resource and Office Administration. Though she was frequently requested to participate in business meetings and press conferences as a senior member of the marketing team, along with employees of different ethnic backgrounds and nationalities, the purpose was primarily to project a positive image of the company to its clients and the media. Apart from these and other occasions when her assistance or presence was required, Kojima has not been considered at all in the many rounds of recruitment by the division.

Her name was also nowhere to be seen on organizational chart, since her position as Senior Manager of Human Resource and Office Administration is to be filled by a new hire when there was sufficient budget. When that happens, Kojima could officially request for a transfer to the marketing department, the CEO had assured her. Kojima was doubtful, but her confidence returned after she was asked to stand in as temporary CEO following her boss' sudden resignation. Kojima assumed the role and responsibilities for more than a year with no additional salary, believing that the rare opportunity might earn her a real promotion one day. While acting as CEO, Kojima was proudly presented as a capable leader and a symbol of modern business practice in a progressive company where there are no gender discriminations. Even so, that did not last either. She was sent back to her former position as soon as a new CEO was hired.

Despite all this, Kojima had remained with the company because she had also been treated rather well, or at least she had thought. She was sent for overseas training, and generous entertainment allowance whenever she was required to be present at business negotiations and meetings. Kojima's employer had also sponsored her golf lessons and contributed partially to the fees of a professional qualification she was encouraged to pursue. These, however, were also the source of her confusion and frustrations. She had often wondered why her employer had treated her fairly well, and yet not taken her career seriously? Was she treated well only because she was a good *tenjihin* (item for display) as a woman? Was her value to the company only as *eien no shokuba no hana* (permanent flower in the workplace)?

For years, Kojima could not decide if she had been unfairly treated, and what course of action she ought to take to redress the situation. She could swallow her pride and allow herself to be showcased by her employer, but the lack of direction in her daily work and the opacity of her career path were unbearably painful. The situation then worsened when a new annual appraisal system was introduced, which triggered a rumour that this was the new CEO's main strategy to replace many employees with his former subordinates at his previous workplace. Under the new appraisal system, Kojima's work performance was to be evaluated by various head of divisions and also by colleagues she worked with. It did not take too long for Kojima to receive conflicting and negative appraisals, which were construed as reflecting a deterioration in the quality of her performance when contrasted against all the impressive work that she had done in the past.

Kojima was eventually asked to leave, though was given a small redundancy package to prevent her from lodging a complaint to the government's labour office about having been unjustly dismissed. What she could and did do was to apply for unemployment allowance from the state to help pay for her living expenses, which for Kojima is more humiliating than being told to resign. To receive the regular income support, she is required to report to the government's labour office every month to report on the progress of her job search, attend training seminars provided by the labour office on how to make job applications, and be interviewed by civil servants to assess Kojima's eligibility for unemployment support. She has said this to me one evening:

> I have never imagined that I would ever be reduced to such a state, and be humiliated in such an extreme way. What is most unbearable is that I have not done anything wrong, but was made to look incapable, useless, and now a destitute. How could I ever find the confidence or courage to walk into another office and do a job properly as a supervisor or manager, when I now know that anyone below and above me could judge my ability on baseless grounds?

The 43-year-old gradually regained her self-confidence after taking a much-needed 'unemployment break' for a year, and found a full-time position as Senior Business Development Manager in a small European company, where she is being treated properly 'as a human' by colleagues with whom she is 'comfortable' working.

Meaningless to be a manager

The kinds of predicaments that Kojima and many women managers have experienced are the main sources of stress and feelings of job insecurity which, in some cases, have led to severe insomnia, emotional depression, psychological disorders, and physical illness that require medical attention and professional help. Nomoto Natsue is yet to seek any professional help, though she often finds herself on the verge of a breakdown due to the excruciating experiences she has had in the office. She has been promoted four times during the 12 years at her current place of employment, but each promotion had come with a prolonged delay in a pay rise that was justified on the grounds of budget cuts due to the Japanese electronics producer's failure to meet its ambitious profit targets. The Senior Finance Manager remembered how quickly her excitement over the news of her first promotion – from Senior Accountant to Assistant Manager – turned into disappointment, dread, and disillusionment when she was informed that her salary would increase by 10 per cent only after she had completed a six-month probation. The actual pay rise came more than a year after her promotion, and in the form of a meagre 5 per cent. She was told the company had under-estimated the costs of acquiring and restructuring a new business, and was experiencing cashflow difficulty. The raise was hardly enough to compensate for the 20-per cent reduction in her monthly intake as a manager. She had put in more overtime hours than before, but was not entitled to full overtime compensation as a member of management. Like many women managers in Japan, Nomoto had to do *sābisu zangyō* (free overtime).

Nomoto remained optimistic, hoping that the next promotion would be different. They were, though, not as she had expected. Not only did each subsequent promotion come with a longer delay in salary increase, but they were in incrementally smaller percentages: 5 per cent for the second promotion, 4 per cent for the third, and 2 per cent for the most recent. Frustrated and angry with yet another *kūkyo shōshin* (empty promotion) the third time, Nomoto tried negotiating for a bigger raise but failed. She asked her superior why her raise was less than those of her peers, and was told that a smaller staff budget was allocated to all back-office divisions including Finance in contrast to revenue-generating divisions such as Sales and Product Development. She was confused, since several male managers in Personnel and Office Administration – both being non-revenue units – each had a bigger percentage increase. This time, her immediate superior's response was a curt 'company policy.' Agitated perhaps by her repeated queries, and to prevent Nomoto from pursuing the matter further, the Finance Director sent the Head of Personnel to reveal the 'truth' to her: several subordinates were said to have each given Nomoto a poor review of her performance as manager for forcing them to work excessively long hours, performing tasks not stated in their job descriptions, hurling verbal abuses at them, and not guiding them well in their daily work.

After consulting with friends and acquaintances, Nomoto approached a local government labour counselling center, and later a labour union's office, for advice on how she could seek redress for unfair treatment by her employer. The government bureau could only advise her to engage the services of a private lawyer, while a union officer cautioned her against taking legal action since the matter could be not easily proven in court, and that a lawsuit could take as long as five years and also seriously jeopardize her future job prospects. The divorced single mother could not afford to take such risks, and so she endured till a new job came along. While she felt trapped in a company where she was under-appreciated and under-valued, Nomoto was more embarrassed to be perceived by her subordinates, peers, and superiors as someone desperate and unable to move elsewhere, despite being a professionally qualified Public Certified Accountant (CPA) and holding a Master's degree in Business Administration (MBA). A male superior had tried to comfort her by advising Nomoto to appreciate the opportunity she had in breaking through the 'glass ceiling' of a company that had made an unprecedented move in making her the first female staff Senior Manager. She would experience the 'problem of gender' anywhere she went, and hence she ought to prioritize her job satisfaction as a female manager and not fuss over a *komakai* (trivial) matter such as asking for a few extra yen to her salary. She had laughed at the irony, and asked herself what satisfaction she could derive when she is not properly paid in her role as manager.

Like many women I have met, Nomoto too has often pondered over what it means to be a *manējā* (manager) or *kanrisha* (a person in managerial position) when her job entails micro-management duties and the performance of menial tasks, while her participation in the activities of the company's upper management is virtually non-existent, and neither has she ever played any role in influencing the business direction of the company. Yet, at the same time, she has to keep spending her own money, time, and energy to keep a job safe. To appease and please her subordinates, for example, Nomoto often pays for the after-work drinking gatherings with them, and works late to complete their share of work so that her subordinates would not have to work late and later complain about her poor time management skills or low EQ (emotional intelligence) for not getting along well with her subordinate. As she said to me recently:

> Nothing makes sense nowadays… since when have managers become slaves serving their subordinates? This is a form of *ijime*, is it not? It is bad enough to be bullied by your peers and superiors, and now we have to tolerate bullying by junior employees too. I have never thought that I was targeted because I am a woman, because other male managers also have similar experience. Is it not meaningless to be a manager or to work when you cannot trust anyone…your employer, your boss and your subordinates?

Nomoto's question about the meaning of being a corporate manager echoes the sentiments of many – if not most – of my informants whose career pursuits have been teeming increasingly with frustrations, confusion, anxiety, insecurity, and despondence. Their experiences can be attributed to varying forms of nominal management, which entailed an empty promotion, reduction in salary due to loss of entitlement to overtime pay, a delay in promotion due to corporate restructuring, a demotion caused by poor performance appraisal, or a combination of these outcomes. Male managers probably also share similar experiences in the current environment of managerial capitalism in Japan. However, women managers are aware of their marginalized position and peripheral role as the 'inferior sex' in the corporate workplace, and often internalize their lesser status out of fear and insecurity that many are more willing to accept and endure some of the unfair practices in the office. This thus makes them susceptible to exploitation, which, in turn, aggravates their situation.

Many of the women managers' experiences described earlier could be construed as forms of workplace bullying and power harassment which, a new law to be implemented in 2020, might offer them some protection and an opportunity to seek compensation. But it remains to be seen if the legislation would be effective. The Japanese government has poor historical records of monitoring corporate activities and imposing penalties that are severe enough to enforce compliance to a given legislation. Nominal management is yet to draw enough attention from the authorities, and the country's antiquated labour laws are also in urgent need of a revision. Then, there is the Equal Employment Opportunity Law[3] (EEOL), which is yet to effect any significant improvement to the working conditions for women since its implementation in 1986. With the persistent lack of strong labour unions in Japan, workers' ability to seek redress through collective representation does not seem optimistic. Furthermore, there are indications that the new legislation might actually have an adverse impact on the working lives of women managers, as we shall see in the next chapter.

Notes

1 According to Article 32 of the Labor Standards Act 1947, an employer 'shall not have a worker work more than 40 hours per week, excluding rest periods' and an employer also 'shall not have a worker work more than 8 hours per day for each day of the week, excluding rest periods.' Article 37 further provides what a worker is entitled to receive for all additional hours worked at a rate that is 'no less than 25 percent and no more than 50 percent over the normal wage per working hour or working day.' However, these provisions do not apply to workers who are 'supervisors' or 'managers' as defined in Article 41.

2 See Chapter 1 for more information about the lack of female participation in the highest level of management in some of the largest publicly listed companies.

3 See Chapter 2 for more discussions on the Equal Employment Opportunity Law (*Danjo Koyō Byōdōhō*) which came into effect on 1 April 1986.

5 To the state

As victims and perpetrators of power harassment

Harassment as a precarious 'game'

'A victim today, a perpetrator tomorrow' is the theme of the television drama *Harassment Game*[1] broadcast by TV Tokyo in October 2018 which could not be truer of the predicament that working adults in Japan are caught in today. As the weekly programme shows, corporate employees relate to one another precariously in the office from day to day as they tread on a tenuous line between appropriate and inappropriate behaviours. Over ten episodes, the drama introduces a wide range of behaviour that would be construed as a form of power harassment or bullying that could lead to a legal suit and also an employee's dismissal. These include *aruhara*[2] (alcohol harassment), *gyakuhara*[3] (reverse harassment), *jendāhara* (gender harassment), *morahara* (moral harassment), *matahara* (maternity harassment, or harassment relating to women's roles as mother), *patahara*[4] (paternity harassment, or harassment relating to men's roles as father), *risuhara*[5] (harassment relating to corporate restructuring), *sekuhara* (sexual harassment), and *sewahara*[6] (sentiment harassment).

The list is aimed at alerting all employees – from the members of the company's board of directors, to the lowest ranked part-time worker – to the need to change their old ways of interacting with every worker by a new Compliance Office which has been formed to enforce the requirements of an impending legislation on curbing workplace bullying and power harassment (*pawā harasumento* or *pawahara*). In doing so, the programme pokes fun at the vagueness and arbitrariness of the definitions of *ijime* (bullying) and *pawahara* in a White Paper released in 2012 ahead of the new legislation. It also highlights the absurdity that the legislation would cause to relations in the workplace as the boundary between appropriate and inappropriate behaviours is increasingly blurred, and also where good and bad behaviours overlap. In each episode of the drama, an employee who claims to be a victim of a form of *pawahara* is easily interpreted as also being guilty of another form of *pawahara*. The most disturbing message delivered by the drama is the recurring note that *pawahara* is like a card game in which all workers – both male and female – could be made victims and also perpetrators, and a game over which they have no control.

This statement both reflects the reality for working adults in Japan today. More importantly, it highlights a radical change to the work environment that further aggravates women's precarious condition. Despite the government's lack of monitoring and enforcement of various existing legislations, two out of the *sanhara* (three forms of harassment) that companies are obliged to train their employees are at least regulated to protect women against certain unfair corporate practices (Shoji 2019). Sexual harassment is regulated by the Equal Employment Opportunity Law 1986 (EEOL), and maternity harassment is governed by the revised Childcare and Nursing Care Leave Law[7] 2017. While power harassment has never been unregulated, due perhaps to many companies' opposition to regulating it, closer attention will be paid to bullying and power harassment in the workplace with the implementation of a new legislation in 2020 (Nikkei 19 November 2018). While women are not specifically targeted by the new law, the broad scope of the legislation and the vague definitions of workplace bullying and *pawahara* are said to have given employers new ways to exploit workers and dismiss undesirable ones, especially those who are older and female (Hsiao 2015; Shoji 2019; Yoshikawa 2017). Women are thus no longer perceived as vulnerable victims, but they are now also vulnerable to being prosecuted as perpetrators.

Discourses on *ijime* and *pawahara* began proliferating in the media, popular literature, public forums, and academic circles in Japan following a survey report issued by the Ministry of Health, Labour and Welfare (MHLW) in 2012. Though the term was said to be first coined by social psychologist Okada Yasuko in 2003 (Roberts 2014: 21), the Tokyo Metropolitan government had in 1995 recognized that workplace bullying and harassment could be legitimate acts for legal action and begun accepting complaints (Hsiao 2015: 183). However, the Japanese government has historically shown reluctance in responding to calls to curb abusive corporate practices. When responses were made, they were at best cosmetic, and at worse countereffective. For over a decade, local government labour offices across Japan had received an increase in reported incidences of workplace *ijime* and *pawahara*, but it was not until the end of 2012 that the labour authorities eventually acknowledged the prevalence of the problems, though this was triggered by the media attention given to the reports of two surveys.

In 2010, the All-Japan Prefectural and Municipal Workers Union (JICHIRO) reported from a survey of approximately 100,000 people that 24.5 per cent of all female respondents had experienced workplace bullying and harassment, while 19.8 per cent of all male respondents had been similar experiences (Naito 2013: 114). A year later, a separate survey conducted by the Japan Institute for Labour Policy and Training (JILPT) showed that there was a 'higher percentage of female victims' of workplace bullying and power harassment, who accounted for 60 per cent of a total of 268 cases received by Japan's prefectural labour bureaus in 2011(Ibid.: 114–5). The report also indicated that the highest incidences were among women in the 40–49 age group, who comprised 26.3 per cent of all 'female victims,' followed by those in the 30–39 age group who accounted for 25.3 per cent (Ibid.). Among the reasons cited were 'overwork and stress caused by staff cuts or too few staff,' 'lack of workplace communication,' and 'results improvement pressure from employers or performance-based system' (Ibid.: 117). However, there was no reference to age, gender, or education as key underlying factors that might have contributed to employees' susceptibility to abuse by employers. Neither reports gave clear indications of whether the victims of abuse were in relatively low job positions within a corporate structure, or if they were in managers being abused by junior employees. The reports also did not mention if the respondents had sought any means of collective action to seek redress or protection, such as enlisting the help of labour unions.

The growing media attention given to these two reports later prompted MHLW to respond with its own survey on some 10,000 individuals. Its report revealed a staggering 139-per cent increase in the number of cases of workplace bullying and power harassment reported to all prefectural labour centres, from 103,194 in 2002 to 246,907 in 2011 (MHLW 2012b: 2). The findings also showed that more full-time employees had experienced bullying and harassment than irregular employees, and that 31.1 per cent of these full-time employees were in managerial positions (Ibid.: 6). However, the report did not provide a detailed breakdown in terms of age, gender, or the nature of their jobs.

Vague definitions and lack of judiciary recognition

As the number of reported cases continued to increase to 254,719 in 2012 (MHLW 2012a), MHLW could no longer ignore the seriousness of workplace bullying and *pawahara* any longer (see Table 5.1). It later made the first attempt at defining workplace *pawahara* in a handbook (MHLW 2013: 2) as

> any conduct directed at a person working in the same workplace by a someone in a position that is superior based on occupational rank, social relations and other factors, which lies beyond the stated scope of a person's job and inflicts emotional distress or physical pain on him/her or makes him/her environment worse.
>
> (Yoshikawa 2017: 532–3)

The handbook identifies six categories of behaviour that could constitute *pawahara*: physical attacks, emotional attacks, isolation from human relationships, excessive demands, demeaning demands, and invasion of privacy (Hsiao 2015: 186–7; MHLW 2013: 5), as shown in Table 5.2. However, the handbook merely offers a limited number of general examples of *pawahara*, and the categories are also rather vague and limited (especially in comparison to the variety and specific types of *pawahara* identified in the drama

Table 5.1 Reported cases of bullying and harassment (2002–2012)

Year	*Number of cases*
2002	1,03,194
2003	1,40,822
2004	1,60,166
2005	1,76,429
2006	1,87,387
2007	1,97,904
2008	2,36,993
2009	2,47,302
2010	2,46,907
2011	2,56,343
2012	2,54,719

Source: The Ministry of Health, Labour and Welfare (2012b: 6).

Harassment Game). The vagueness allows employers to exploit the situation instead of helping to prevent abusive practices against employees. MHLW's recommendations to employers to not exert 'excessive work demands' on employees, for example, are justifiable if the assigned tasks could be proven to facilitate an employee's career development. This leaves employers and employees to argue and determine what constitute as 'excessive work demands' and 'demeaning workload,' which defeats the purpose of having a new legislation to curb bullying and harassment. Also, the handbook made no attempt to link abusive behaviours to cultural factors such as age and gender.

Other than suggesting to employers to raise awareness through staff training and corporate announcements, MHLW did not indicate if or how the state would regulate and discipline companies for not having adequate preventive measures, let alone stipulate the forms of penalty or punishment should abuse arise. The lack of clarity and the silence on specific matters could easily be construed as signs of official endorsement and encouragement of corporate abuse. At the same time, they could also be a timely and much-needed opportunity for some employees to utilize the new legislation against their co-workers, as a way of venting their pent-up anger with unfairness in the workplace and also their frustrations with various problems generated by the increasingly flexible work environment. The new discourses on *ijime* and *pawahara* could thus be a convenient tool to legitimize diverse practices that point to larger socio-economic issues.

Most significantly, the examples listed by MHLW are said to 'deficient,' as they are not acts that are recognized by the judiciary in Japan as forms of power harassment that could be addressed properly in court in the event of an appeal or legal suit (Hsiao 2015: 187–8). Power harassment is also not defined as an act that could be judged in a Civil Court under Tort Law[8] (Ibid.: 188). What this means is that an employee could file a complaint with

Table 5.2 Classification of power harassment by The Ministry of Health, Labour and Welfare (MHLW)

Category	*Examples (for victims)*
Physical attacks Assaults and various acts of violence	Being yelled at Being kicked or hit Being harmed by something being thrown at
Emotional attacks Threats, character assassination, insults, and cruelty	Being reprimanded in front of others Being verbally abused or called names Being told that he or she is incompetent
Isolation from human relationships Being ignored, alienated, and segregated	Being ignored Being alienated by others who have been instructed to not extend any assistance Being intentionally omitted from activities with other colleagues
Excessive demands Being assigned unnecessary or impossible tasks that interfere with normal work	Being given heavy workload, especially when it is at the end of the work day Being given too many tasks that require constant use of time outside the office Being told to complete tasks beyond the ability of one person
Demeaning demands Being assigned low-level tasks unrelated to job, duties, experience, and abilities	Being assigned menial tasks that are beneath one's position or rank Being forced during working hours to run errands and trivial tasks Being assigned menial tasks that are beneath one's position or rank
Intrusion into privacy Excessive interference with one's private life	Being asked personal questions Being probed and commented about one's private life Being criticized for one's attire, ethnicity, gender, or religion in front of others

Sources: Compiled from MHLW (2013: 5), with translation of texts modified from Philip Hsiao (2015: 186–7).

the government's labour office about having been bullied or subject to *pawa-hara* in the office, but since courts in Japan do not have a clear definition of which specific forms of workplace bullying and power harassment are actionable, the employee thus risks having the case be judged arbitrarily with little or no certainty of the outcome of a judge's ruling.

However, the Japanese government had been under a lot of pressure by the public to address the rising incidence of *karōshi* (death as a result of overwork) and suicides due to bullying and harassment. MHLW was thus compelled to introduce some measures to combat these practices, or merely to show that they are doing something to tackle the issues. The number of deaths by suicide in Japan might have decreased from 30,000 in 1998, but there were 20,431 suicides in 2017 (SHJ 2018: 167), which ranked the country 7th among OECD countries with the world's highest suicide rates that year (OECD 2017: 61). Many court cases had in the past concluded with employees failing to sue their employers for bullying or harassment, though several recent rulings had been in the favour of the claimants. While detailed information about the causes of suicides is difficult to obtain, media coverage of some recent cases of suicides due to *karōshi*, *ijime*, and *pawahara* had sparked many public debates and forums calling for the state to resolve the problem of long working hours, prevent workplace bullying, and punish employers for harassing employees.

A court in Nagoya awarded the widow of an employee a labour insurance payout after ruling that the deceased had been committed suicide after he was severely bullied in the office, where his superior had imposed excessively high workload on him, and reproached him in front of co-workers (Hsiao 2015: 189). In 2007, an Osaka court ordered for damages to be paid to the family of an employee who had committed suicide after he had been openly humiliated by his superior in front of the company's high-level executives at a public event (Ibid.). Perhaps the most prominent case was that of a male nurse who had taken his own life after he was verbally abused by a senior nurse in front of other co-workers and repeatedly forced to run errands for his superior – including taking care of his child, washing his car, queuing on his behalf at amusement centres, picking him up from brothels, and paying for drinking activities with superiors – which led a court in Saitama in 2012 to award damages for the family of the deceased (Ibid.).

But these cases were extreme cases of individuals who had lost their lives, and among only a few that had been ruled in favour of the victims' family. MHLW is yet to impose any strict measures to punish corporations for violating labour laws. When penalties were imposed, they were so minuscule and negligible that the exercises seemed to be nothing more than a gentle slap on the wrist, or they were not publicized at all. In 2016, Yamamoto Toshihiro, the President and CEO of Japan's largest advertising agency Dentsu, publicly admitted that his company had illegally forced several employees to work long hours which had led to the suicide of the 24-year-old female employee Takahashi Matsuri in 2015. However, the prosecutors only imposed a fine of 500,000 yen ($4,603, or £3,795) on the company for failing to correct its illegal labour practices (Kawasaki 2016). In the same year, Japan's largest state-run broadcasting company NHK also admitted having made a 31-year-old female reporter work 159 hours of overtime in a month with only two days off and for eventually causing her death in 2013, though the government's labour office's final conclusion in 2014 was not made public (Adelstein 2017). Official statistics on *karōshi* and suicides caused by bullying and harassment are difficult to obtain, though some estimated that 2,000 *karōshi* claims are made annually for government compensation, of which approximately 37 per cent were successful (BBC 6 October 2017).

Corporate compliance for image enhancement

Amid increasing public pressure, Prime Minister Abe Shinzo had quickly endorsed a plan for sweeping reforms of workplace practices, including placing limits on overtime hours, and improving wages for contract workers. Without a clear monitoring system or strict implementation of punitive measures, however, all the action taken by MHLW could not effectively combat the various problems that workers experience in the office (Kyodo 2019). From my field data, I gathered that companies could easily circumvent any new regulations by, for example, coercing or blackmailing employees to not report on overtime hours, or by offering empty promotions in lieu of salary increase that both regular and irregular employees desire, need, and would willingly accept, as discussed in Chapter 4.

In preparation for the impending legislation on preventing workplace bullying and power harassment, many employers have made scrambled to set up a compliance office or expand one, and also publishing compliance manuals or updating old ones. How each company actually monitors and implements change is difficult to assess. A quick survey I made of the published compliance manuals of publicly listed companies in Japan showed that these materials contain minimal explanations on bullying and harassment. In the 40-page compliance manual of one company, for example, there is only one short sentence which states that the company 'prohibits directors and employees from engaging in any form of abuse or harassment.' NSK Limited, a large Japanese manufacturer of bearings and heavy industrial equipment, is obliged by being a listed company on the Tokyo Stock Exchange and a component of the Nikkei 225 stock index to openly publish its staff compliance guide online for investors and the public. The guide contains long lists of prohibited acts for the company's 30,000 employees, though is silent on how employees could report on any violation of the rules. Similarly, the publicly available compliance manuals of other companies such as Daiwa Securities, Fujifilm Holdings, Marubeni Group, Mizuho Financial Group, Mitsui & Company, NEC Group, Sekisui Chemical Company, Sony Corporation, Sumitomo Corporation, and Yamaha Corporation also contain lists of prohibited and required behaviour, with several companies providing details on the procedures employees could take to report on violations to the respective companies' rules, though several others make no mention at of bullying or power harassment.

Compliance departments may have sprouted everywhere, and compliance manuals are available for employees to know what behaviour would be appropriate or inappropriate, but it is difficult to ascertain if the actual execution and handling of incidents relating to workplace bullying and *pawahara* are not arbitrary, or still subject to various existing assumptions and culturally constituted notions of what is good or appropriate behaviour and also on prevailing perceptions of age and gender. Based on a quick survey of 30 companies that I conducted, several senior executives admit that their employers lack experience in managing such behaviours. A few directors acknowledge that their companies are not well-equipped to train their employees to properly understand that certain historically permissible behaviours would now be deemed as forms of workplace bullying and *pawahara*. The compliance officers of two large Japanese corporations explain that their employers have long implemented strong internal measures to prevent, manage, and resolve bullying and harassment among workers. However, among the biggest difficulties they have experienced are disciplining members of the senior management who are themselves often the worse bullies and the main sources of harassment, and hence set examples for lower-ranked managers to emulate. Yet, the officers of all 30 companies concur that employers largely welcome the opportunity to enhance their corporate image by improving on their compliance system to curb workplace bullying and harassment. But since the requirements stipulated by MHLW are unclear and arbitrary, companies could also take advantage of the vagueness of these measures to dismiss workers who are deemed 'undesirable.'

Legitimizing workplace bullying and power harassment

If working under such circumstance is difficult, being a corporate manager could lead one to face considerable risk, especially when one is female or advanced in age. Given also that union membership in Japan is small, and labour unions are historically weak in offering workers adequate collective representation, women's position as corporate managers could be made more precarious. The following cases will demonstrate the various predicaments of several women managers.

An age of terror

Sano Sayaka had settled fairly comfortably in her new job as Senior Management Consultant in a European company when I last met her in Tokyo in 2019. The 48-year-old looked relaxed, and had a certain glow on her face which I had not seen for many years until that day. She seemed to have recovered fully from a tormenting experience in 2016 which had made her lose all confidence in herself as she cried every night to sleep. At times, she had felt so helpless and miserable that she came close to ending her life. But I was glad to see the lively, confident, and humorous Sano again that summer. As we talked at length again about 'the most ludicrous experience' she had at her former workplace, I recalled how unusually gaunt, pale, and despondent she looked when I saw her in 2016. She was 'under house arrest' back then, as she had described her situation. Sano had been at home for several months while she waited for the legal representative from a labour union's office to finalize a negotiation with her employer at that time. Though she was being paid her usual salary, Sano was not allowed to be in the office, and also denied access to all the files in her office computer. All she could do was to wait for a deal to be negotiated, which eventually lasted a total of ten months.

It all happened one early morning when Sano arrived at the office to find the head of human resource waiting at her desk. After they were seated alone in a conference room, he informed her that orders had come from the top that Sano must leave her position as Treasury and Management Accounting Manager and choose one out of three alternatives. One was to resign immediately with a severance package amounting to two months of her gross salary, before tax and pension deductions. The second was to transfer to a different division in the same office where she would be stripped of the title of manager, become an ordinary employee, and have her salary reduced by 25 per cent. The third was to work in a branch office outside Tokyo – a two-hour commute from her home – and work as Recruitment Consultant responsible for helping individuals with disabilities find employment, and take a 30-per cent pay cut. What had she done to deserve this, she had asked. The human resource manager's response was that the Chief Finance Officer (CFO), whom Sano had often disagreed with, had received complaints from several junior employees about Sano's 'bad attitude' towards them, which they had described as acts of *pawahara*. When the confused Sano asked for more information, he refused to divulge the names of these junior employees, or cite any specific incident. Sano was given a week to decide, though he strongly advised her to accept the first option and resign immediately, since she now had a tarnished reputation in the office, and poor relations with co-workers.

How could she possibly have abused her position of power when she had none to begin with, she was befuddled. Since joining the company in 2004, Sano's own team shrunk from eight to two by upper management after several rounds of budget cuts. The only subordinate she had was forced to quit after the company refused to extend the part-time worker's contract. Sano had been a leader of a team with no member for a year. She knew that the company had distributed most of the accounting functions to various other divisions and removed all her subordinates so that she would eventually be frustrated and resign on her own accord. But Sano had refused to budge. Instead, she endured being a 'manager-at-large' by liaising with colleagues in different divisions, handling a variety of ad-hoc assignments and menial tasks which were intended for low-level employees, and also having to complete other managers' work. She had often thought of resigning, but did not wish to do so until she could secure a better job elsewhere. While she had contacted several recruitment agencies to help her find another job, no offer had come her way.

The meeting with the human resource manager made Sano furious and confused. She had enough, and would not be bullied any further by the company. Against the earnest persuasions of her husband, siblings, and friends, Sano braced herself for an ugly confrontation with her employer as she made her way to a government labour bureau and workers' union. To her relief, both offices confirmed that hers was a case of *ijime* or *pawahara*, and that she could be entitled to sue her employer for compensation under the new initiative introduced by MHLW. Yet, Sano was unsure about the outcome, worrying if the court ruling could be in favour of the company, which was often the case in Japan. If that was the case, she would lose her job and also be blacklisted by recruitment agencies. Prospective employers typically avoid hiring someone who is a labour union member. A person who has taken legal action against an employer would certainly not be considered at all. Agencies would, therefore, not forward to clients the resume of such a person as a potential candidate.

Also, legal proceedings in Japan are notoriously lengthy, lasting two years or more. This meant that Sano would have to remain in her current workplace and endure the gossips, which would aggravate her humiliation and anger until the case was resolved. A mutual friend Okada Omi beseeched Sano to not pursue the matter when we had dinner together one evening in 2016. 'Don't be a fool! Forget about the legal action and just move on!' Okada had said, as she reflected on her own experience. She lost her job a year earlier after her employer of five years announced another budget cut, and hired a less-experienced but younger and cheaper female to replace Okada as Investor Relations Manager. Out of anger over the unjust treatment, Okada had gone to the labour union office and the local labour bureau for advice and assistance, but later withdrew her request. She devoted herself instead to preparing for her next job, ploughing her savings into an expensive training course to enhance her self-image, and a professional workshop to help her cope with her bruised self-esteem. Okada eventually found a job as Director of Corporate Communications, but it was a nice-sounding title that paid a fraction of her former income. She had settled for less, though was relieved she did not have to go through a legal ordeal had she filed a suit against her former employer. Her advice to her friend Sano was:

> There is no point in fighting for our rights. We are powerless. We are living in an age of terror, when the winners are the strong ones with big weapons. We are little women who will always lose against big and powerful institutions. They will always win. The government and the legal system are on their side. No one is on ours. Only useless labour unions with no power to do anything but complain. To stay in the game (of work), we have to fend for ourselves and keep the union out of the game. Do not waste your time and energy fighting. Use them on finding your next job…

Sano had received a similar advice from her husband Haruto whose main concern was that a drawn-out legal battle might adversely affect his own job. Given the prominence of Sano's employer, the case might be in the news. If her name was mentioned, then everyone in his office would know that it was his wife who had taken on a giant Japanese company. Haruto was afraid that this could reflect badly on him, and even cost him his job.

After spending many sleepless nights mulling over the matter, Sano decided to go ahead with her initial plan. She paid 200,000 yen ($1,950, or £1,520) for professional legal fees for private consultations on the litigation process, and prepared herself to sacrifice all her savings in the event that she had to pay further legal costs. What terrified her the most was finding sufficient money should she lose the legal battle, and be ordered to pay damages to her employer. Sano was unconcerned about receiving a compensation from her employer, her future job prospects, or negotiating for a bigger redundancy package. It was also not audacity, determination, or stubbornness that had driven her to take this course of action, as most of her friends had assumed. Rather, as she explained to me at that time:

> I desperately need to restore my bruised self-esteem, regain my self-confidence, and find some shred of hope that there is still justice in this world, and meaning in life. That I have lost all this made me feel fearless. I am not fighting against the company. I am fighting for hope, meaning, and my life. If I do not do this, then I might as well not live...

She would be sad to lose her marriage, though her husband eventually assured her that he would support her all the way, and hoped that Sano might encourage many workers in Japan to also not be afraid to take action against abusive corporate practices.

As soon as the negotiation began, Sano's employer demanded that she worked from home, even though she was not given anything to do, except for taking telephone calls and responding to emails using her own personal account. She was also not allowed to travel, engage in any job-hunting activity, or take up a part-time job. Sano described those months as unbearably exasperating and extremely stressful, likening her situation to that of someone being put 'under house arrest.' Her legal representative later informed Sano that while it was illegal for companies in Japan to dismiss employees without giving a month's notice, this could be done if the employer could prove the employee's misconduct. Her employer seemed to have gathered 'proofs' from many more employees of Sano's abusive behaviour towards them. I could remember how heartily she had laughed as she told me about some of the 'ridiculously bizarre proof' her employer had fabricated. One statement was written and signed by a co-worker whom Sano hardly knew but who said that Sano had deliberately ignored the co-worker despite being greeted repeatedly, and had hence made the co-worker feel alienated. Another was made by a young male employee who said that Sano had made advances at him, stood very close to him while they were discussing work, and even touched him his hand on many occasions. As Sano had assumed, a co-worker with whom she was on friendly terms with later explained that several junior employees had been instructed to write the statements or risk losing their job. Though Sano's legal adviser assured her that the statements were baseless and would not hold up in court, she could not help but feel sorry that these young co-workers had been bullied by the company as she herself had. She had said to me:

> We are living in confusing and dangerous times. The government wants to show that it is doing something about many problems in companies,

> but it does not really want to solve them properly. Companies are using scapegoats to show that they are minimizing power harassment and bullying in the office that anyone can now be accused of power harassment over a trivial matter. Sometimes companies fake situations and create evidence to support their lies. Nobody knows how to behave in the office anymore.

After learning from the labour union's lawyer that her employer's proposal to cut Sano's salary would exceed the legal limit of 10 per cent, she carefully deliberated over the course of action that she wanted, and eventually sought her legal representative's help to inform the company that she would accept the option to be transferred to a newly established branch office outside Tokyo, where she would work as Recruitment Consultant to help individuals with disabilities find employment. She was prepared to accept a five-per cent pay cut, but there was to be no change to all other benefits. Sano also demanded a written statement from the company to clarify that the transfer was her own decision, and that there was to be no mention of any abuse against her co-workers in her employment records. She would divulge all the details to the media should the company refuse to agree with any of these terms.

She later learned from several colleagues that her decision had shocked the senior management and frustrated the CFO who had devised this scheme to dismiss Sano. Her proposal was accepted a month later, by which time the CFO had also been replaced. The latter gave Sano much relief. She was more pleased, though, to move into a new line of work in which she had no experience in, and which was to later enable her to secure her present job. Most of all, Sano could comfort herself by the thought that she had helped hundreds of disabled people find jobs during the two years she spent in the branch office. Her decision had also surprised the legal representative and several labour union officers, who had initially thought Sano was silly to take on such an arduous battle, and even insane to accept the worst of the three options. They could have negotiated for a better compensation package had she agreed to resign, which was the normal course of action for most individuals who had consulted the union. But they later found her refusal to succumb to the 'game' played by the company to turn her from a victim into a perpetrator of *pawahara* admirable, especially for having set a precedence for many workers. As the labour union officer in charge of Sano's case said:

> I have handled many cases over the years but I have never seen anyone as determined and strong as her [Sano] in fighting for her self-esteem and self-pride. Most people want to be compensated, or to shame their employer for the abuses they have suffered. She wants to be neither a victim or perpetrator of *ijime* and *pawahara*. She was seriously crushed. The state of her emotional and mental health was so bad that she could not function properly. She needed to regain her self-confidence, and

> find some justice amidst the wrongdoings by her employer, so that she could be a whole person again…

All that certainly came at a high, incalculable cost for Sano. Until today, she could still vividly remember the embarrassment and shame she had felt after being told that she was to resign or accept one of the three options. Since the company took more than a month to issue a formal letter, Sano could not consult the government's labour office or a workers' union sooner. She had to endure many weeks of pain and humiliation in the office with no work to do but endless questioning by co-workers, and also with the human resource manager pestering her on a daily basis to make a decision. Sano has to live with the traumatic experience for a very long time.

Limited legal provisions on dismissals

Very few employees are like Sano who would dare to take the risks she did. Sano is indeed rare. Many other informants in this study may have also experienced various forms of *pawahara* in the workplace, but most would rather ignore and endure, for fear of losing their job. This stems from their perceptions of the labour laws in Japan as biased towards employers and against workers, contrary to general views that the country's employment laws make it impossible to dismiss regular workers (Sugeno and Yamakoshi 2014a: 83). Revisions have been made to the labour laws in Japan over the past hundred years in governing the dismissal of workers, and the burden of proof lies on the employer in the case of a dispute. But the legislations still remain rather vague, which allow large corporations with a strong legal team to interpret specific situations and argue in their own favour.

The labour laws in Japan are based on the Civil Code established by the Meiji government in 1896, which had provided that an employer or employee could terminate a contract of employment by giving two weeks' advance notice, and was silent on abusive or unfair dismissal (Ibid.: 83). When the postwar Labour Standards Act (LSA) came into force in 1947 to incorporate the Civil Code, the two-week dismissal notice period was extended to 30 days. While employers continued to have the freedom to dismiss workers (Kambayashi 2010: 8), the new Labour Union Act (LUA) introduced in the same year stipulated that the dismissal of workers who were labour union members would be an unfair labour practice. This perhaps explains why some employers in Japan have avoided hiring workers who are union members, and many still do so today. In 1986, the EEOL was implemented to regulate the hiring, unfair treatment, and dismissal of workers based on gender discriminations. Though minor revisions were made to the LSA in 2003, the lack of clarity on unfair and abusive dismissals has led judges to make rulings based on case laws that have been established by various district courts since 1945. Over time, the collection of case laws has come to be known as *Kaikoken Ranyō Hōri*, translated as the Legal Doctrine of

Abusive Dismissals (Ibid.: 7). Some of these case laws were later included in the Labour Contract Act (LCA) in 2007 which incorporated the revised LSA in 2003, and gave more clarity to the regulations on the dismissal of workers on grounds relating to gender, nationality, pregnancy, and family care (Sugeno and Yamakoshi 2014a: 84).

More importantly, the LCA 2007 specifies four categories of 'reasons' for dismissals, some of which are subject to various interpretations and hence highly contentious. One is the expiration of a worker' contract of employment, which the employer is not required to offer any explanation for not renewing or extending it. The second is dismissal on the grounds of the employee's misconduct, which includes negligence of duties, defiance, disobedience, violation of discipline, or infringement of the employer's reputation, as stated in the company's compliance manual and staff regulations. An employer is required to issue warnings, suspend a worker's employment, or 'negotiate' the latter's resignation on a voluntary basis. Employees are also to be given an 'acceptable' compensation which may include a lump-sum payment equivalent to several months' salary and any other accrued payments and benefits. The third category of reasons is dismissal on the ground that an employee is incapable of performing his or her designated duties as a result of injury, illness, prolonged absence from work (because of disappearance or confinement due to criminal charges), or poor job performance (due to lack of professional qualifications or experience). Some of these supposed reasons can be highly contentious, and could also place corporate managers in a particularly vulnerable position. When employees receive a promotion, for example, they often assume more responsibilities that are new and unfamiliar to their previous scope of work. Some may be transferred to positions or lines of work that are unrelated to their fields of specialization which require skills beyond their professional training. An employer wishing to dismiss an undesirable worker could easily promote the latter only to evaluate the employee's job performance negatively. At the same time, the company could easily defend itself by explaining the promotion as recognition of the employee's good performance in the past, and as reward for career advancement, which the employee is unable to live up to.

The fourth reason for dismissal is on grounds of a company's economic circumstances, that is, an employer needs to plan for collective redundancy due to financial difficulties. A company is required to demonstrate the necessity of reducing its workforce to avoid insolvency, and also explain the selection criteria for dismissing specific workers, which have in recent years readily received the state's endorsement (Sugeno and Yamakoshi 2014b: 121). However, the legislation does not impose on employers any requirement to produce a detailed plan for minimizing the hardship caused to workers due to mass layoffs, nor does it require companies to offer any severance pay (Sugeno and Yamakoshi 2014a: 87–8). At the same time, the state offers employers partial reimbursement of the expenses for hiring private agencies to offer displaced workers re-employment support (OECD 2018: 150). While

Table 5.3 Four-stage procedures for resolving labour disputes over dismissals

Stage	*Place where disputes are handled*	*Disputes handled in 2012*	*% of total*
1. Information and Consultation Services	MHLW's Regional Administrative Office	51,515	*100.0*
2. Conciliation Services	MHLW's Regional Administrative Office	1,904	*3.7*
3. Tribunal Procedure	The District Court	1,735	*3.4*
4. Civil Litigation	The District Court, the High Court, and the Supreme Court	1,026	*2.0*

Sources: Compiled from Kazuo Sugeno and Keiichi Yamakoshi (2014a: 91) with modifications by the author.

employees who are union members could negotiate through collective bargaining with the help of their respective labour unions, others could report to the labour office and undergo the necessary legal procedures to resolve any disputes arising from unfair or abusive dismissal, as Sano did.

However, the procedures for resolving disputes on dismissal comprise four stages (see Table 5.3), which can be arduously long and tedious. The first stage is a free assessment of a worker's grievance over an unfair dismissal by a regional labour administrative office under MHLW that offers 'Information and Consultation Services.' The employer may be requested to discuss and resolve the dispute informally only after the administrative office has established a worker's dispute to be valid. The second stage is that of 'Conciliation Services' rendered by the regional labour administrative office, which would form a panel – comprising its own officers, practising lawyers and other legal professionals – to reach a settlement between a worker and the employer. The cases resolved in this phase tend to be small, and typically involve less than 400,000 yen ($3,683, or £3,036) in monetary settlements (Ibid.: 89).

MHLW would no longer be involved in unresolved disputes that proceed to the third stage, which would enter the judiciary system governed by the Labour Tribunal Act (LTA) of 2004. This legislation allows a dispute to be heard and determined in a district court by a labour tribunal comprising a judge and two 'part-time experts in labour relations' (Ibid.). A maximum of three sessions or hearings is stipulated by the LTA, after which an unresolved dispute would be automatically transferred to the formal Civil Procedure. Since there is no statute of limitation for disputes arising from abusive or unfair dismissals provided by the Code of Civil Procedure (CCP) of 1998, a civil case could last several years, with both the employee and the employer bearing the cost of their own legal advisers. In the meantime, the employer is required to pay the employee's salary throughout the entire procedure which might help the latter partially meet his or her legal expense.

According to official data, a total of 51,515 labour disputes over unfair or abusive dismissals were reported to MHLW's administrative offices in 2012. The Conciliation phase resolved 1,904 cases (3.7 per cent), while 1,735 disputes (3.4 per cent) were transferred to the Tribunal, of which 1,026 cases (2.0 per cent) were handled by the Civil Court (Ibid.: 90–1). Out of the total number of cases reported that year, settlements through negotiations amounted to 3,668 (7.2 per cent), while 166 disputes (0.3 per cent) were ruled in favour of the employee in civil litigation (Ibid.: 91). These statistics are for rough reference, as details on the employees' profiles such as gender, age, occupation, and employment sector are unavailable. Yet, they do highlight the difficulties encountered by workers in taking legal action against their respective employers on grounds of unfair dismissal. This perhaps accounts for why approximately half of disputed cases were historically settled privately or outside the judiciary system. As a survey by JILPT showed, approximately half of all disputes on dismissal reported to MHLW between 2007 and 2012 were resolved through private negotiations between employees and employers (Sugeno and Yamakoshi 2014b: 126). Of these, many were said to be mediated by labour unions which typically tended to avoid the lengthy and complicated legal procedures (Ibid.).

Labour unions in disunion

Labour unions in Japan, however, are known for their increasingly marginalized role in fighting for workers' rights and diminished ability to provide workers with adequate collective representation (Gagné 2018: 69; Gordon 2008: 247). As a study in 2010 showed, the total number of 26,000 unions together had ten million full-time workers as affiliated members, representing a union participation rate of 18.5 per cent (Fujimura 2012: 6–7). That was a sharp decline from a record high of 55.8 per cent in 1949, and from 30 per cent between the 1950s and 1970s (Ibid.: 7). The unionization rate among part-time workers was considerably lower, at 2.6 per cent in 2000, and increasing only slightly to 5.6 per cent in 2010. Part-time workers constituted approximately 2.3 per cent of all unionized workers in 2000, and 7.0 per cent in 2009 (Ibid.). This is because enterprise unions are formed by and for individual companies, and historically organized for only regular workers, who used to comprise a large majority of a company's workforce in the past (Ibid.: 10). Despite the expansion of irregular workers in post-bubble Japan, enterprise unions still do not consider themselves as representatives of part-time and contract workers, and are thus labelled as unions for a 'labour aristocracy' (Broadbent 2010: 217). The country's largest is the Japanese Trade Union Confederation (*Nihon Rōdōkumiai Sōrengōkai*), commonly referred to as RENGO, which has since its foundation in 1987 not been effective in lobbying for positive changes to labour policies and practices, but successful on occasions only in opposing the passing of certain legislations that might have negative effects on workers (Nakamura 2007: 11).

Moreover, most labour unions in Japan are run by men, who are said to have the tendency of not taking the predicaments of female workers seriously, due to historically constructed cultural perceptions of women's work as being less important than that of their male counterparts (Broadbent 2010: 217). While several women-only unions have emerged to represent female workers, they are small, independent entities whose operations are separate from those of large union federations and enterprise unions, and hence they do not have a strong voice. The country's first women-only union *Onna Rōdō Kumiai Kansai* (Kansai Labour Union for Women), or *Onna Kumiai*, was formed in 1990 by female workers. By 2003, there were 12 women-only unions, of which the largest is *Josei Union Tokyo* (Women's Union Tokyo) with 250 members (Ibid.: 213). *Onna Kumiai*, for example, is run by volunteers who have their own full-time job and hence could spare little time to recruiting new members and managing the union's activities. While *Josei Tokyo* was formed and is still being managed by two full-time executive members, the union trains and encourages its members to resolve their own individual problems as far as possible, based on the union's philosophy of 'by members, for members' (Ibid.: 225). Though these women's unions have over the years worked in coalition to help female workers fight and win disputes with employers, they are still far from a long way from being powerful entities with a strong collective voice.

Among the many difficulties faced by all the labour unions in Japan is the perception of their ineffectiveness in representing workers' interests and pushing for positive change persists; workers are more encouraged to enlist the help from unions, hence fuelling the vicious cycle of weakening their effectiveness even more (Mabuchi 2007: 99). The situation is complicated further by the incredulously long and costly litigation process under Japan's antiquated and bureaucratic legal system. This is perhaps why many workers in Japan avoid labour unions. Some are afraid; others find them incapable of helping. More importantly, most employees perceive their experiences as either too trivial to deserve the attention of a union's assistance, or that they are difficult to prove. This was the case for Murata Mayo.

A boat lost in a storm without a compass

The 46-year-old currently works as Customer Services and Relations Manager for a large retail company. This is a new field for her. She would not have chosen this line of work had she not been forced to resign from her former job as Head of Administrative Affairs in a large Japanese bank, where she had worked for more than 15 years. Like Sano, Murata also had a rather traumatic experience. But unlike Sano, she was too afraid to take any action or seek any assistance. Despite being in charge of her division, Murata was not always treated with respect by her male superiors, nor taken seriously by several peers and subordinates. Being amiable, obliging, and helpful, Murata was often asked to run errands for her superiors. A few had also made passes at her. Perhaps she had worked in the company for a long time, and co-workers who had risen in the ranks together with her still treated her as they knew her when she first joined the company. She could not recall how it all started, though she remembered the day when a director who had known her for many years asked for her help to tidy up his office. His secretary was on maternity leave. The temporary assistant was too young, inexperienced, and disorganized that she could neither find documents he needed, nor was she bothered to keep the office tidy. His request, however, was not only to re-file documents, but to also re-arrange items in his office refrigerator, and to ensure that regular orders were made for all his desired drinks and snacks.

Murata had assumed that the request would be temporary, but it persisted. Even after the director's secretary had returned to work, the director insisted on having Murata continue with the many menial tasks. It has pleased him that she performed those tasks so well, he had said. The demands gradually increased to include picking up his dry-cleaning; sending his shoes to be polished; making travel arrangements and hotel room reservations on his behalf using Murata's name; and also buying and keeping a record of all the gifts for his wife and female companions. She had gently expressed her wish for him to stop after a year, but his response was always: 'This is a compliment…I ask you to do these because I trust you.'

While Murata was upset that the director had confused her job as head of administration with that of his personal assistant and secretary, his abusive behaviour had set a precedence for two other executive directors to follow. Soon, she had to also do grocery shopping, arrange for domestic cleaners, pick up children, and even run errands for the wives and mistresses of these directors. She had spent so much on unrelated, private activities that she could not perform her own job in office administration properly, which eventually affected her performance evaluations. Instead of standing up for her or overlooking the matter, the superiors whom she had been running errands for supported a decision by the human resource manager to issue Murata a warning for her poor work performance.

Once again, she spoke to the director who had started the abusive treatment. This time, Murata was told that she had willingly performed all the personal and private arrangements. Perhaps she had wanted to gain favour from her superiors. It was her fault and hers alone that she had neglected her own work as head of office administration. The menial tasks suddenly stopped. All the three directors had also avoided making eye contact with or greeting Murata. She felt relieved, and thought she could finally get back to doing her own job properly, but the following performance appraisal came with a worse assessment of her work, a stronger warning, and a one-month probation for Murata to show improvement or be dismissed on grounds of her being no longer capable of doing her job.

She had refrained from filing a complaint to the government's labour office about the unrelated personal errands she was asked to do, for fear that she would be laughed at. Now she could not tolerate any longer, and mustered the courage to report to a labour office. Unfortunately, she was told that she did not have a case. There was no evidence of her having been abused. She had not been physically harmed or suffered personal injuries. She had also not been medically certified as suffering from emotional depression or a mental breakdown. Humiliated and angry, Murata went to another labour office, hoping that she might meet a more compassionate civil servant who would be willing to accept her complaint. After she was given a similar response, Murata realized that government offices did not wish to record incidents such as those she had experienced. Unwilling to give up, she consulted a private lawyer specializing in labour disputes, and was again told that she did not have a case. Murata had not filed a complaint while she was being told to perform the range of personal tasks for the directors, and had done so only after her work performance had deteriorated, he had said. The director was probably right. She had acted willingly, and there was no evidence of bullying or harassment, and so Murata would not be able to convince any judge. On the contrary, she might be humiliated further should she lose the legal suit. As her husband did, the lawyer advised her too not to think of her experiences as embarrassing or humiliating, but to accept them as what *sararīman* in Japan often have to do to keep their job and move on. By then, Murata really felt that she was on the brink of emotional depression or a breakdown, and also driven to the precipice that she might as well commit suicide and finally produce the necessary 'evidence' of the abusive practices she had been subjected to. But the evidence had come too late. She did not have a case.

It was unbearable to remain any longer with the company. Those years she had spent running errands for the various directors had triggered rumours about Murata sleeping with her superiors in exchange for career advancement. Since the errands involved private matters, Murata had also not divulged to anyone in the office. Moreover, none of the directors had treated her badly in front of others; no one in the office could support her claims of having been bullied or harassed by them. What was apparent to her co-workers was that Murata's work performance had indeed deteriorated. There was hence little she could do but to resign, and hope that she could gradually recover from the humiliation and abuse. She walked out of her job, and later her marriage. She was to spend two years in therapy before she could pull herself together to find a new job. She still blames herself today for what happened, as she explained when we met in 2019:

> What they did to me was awful. I wish I had acted sooner. It was my fault. It was all my fault. I was too naïve, too gullible, and too trusting. My bosses had abused me because I let them. I let them because I was a coward. And I was a coward because I did not want to lose my job. How

> could anyone say no to their bosses? What could employees do when their superiors have so much power to destroy their jobs and their lives? I was so lost, like a boat lost in a storm without a compass in the middle of the ocean. I did not know where to go or what to do. Who could have helped me?

A demanding mental health certification process

Murata's case would indeed be difficult to prove in court without the necessary evidence of workplace bullying and power harassment. Even if she could produce some, legal provisions in Japan only allow for medical treatment and compensation entitlement relating only to mental disorders. Since power harassment is also not a legal term, a victim of power harassment who does not suffer from any mental disorder is not entitled to receive payment for treatment of emotional distress or depression. MHLW acknowledged in a survey made in 2007 that 'problems of human relationships in the workplace' are key contributors to intense anxiety, worries, and stress over work and occupational lifestyles which could lead to mental health problems and the cost of medical treatment for which would be covered by social insurance, as well as compensation of loss of earnings (Mizushima 2013: 40). Even so, the procedures for making claims and receiving compensation are rather long and complicated. MHLW revised the guidelines for the identification and treatment of mental health problems due to work-related stress by issuing the 'Certification Criteria for Mental Disorders Caused by Psychological Stress' in 2011. An employee will be assessed by a professional qualified psychiatrist through a series of screening and consultations, as well as a stringent method of evaluation, before being certified as a 'strong,' 'medium,' or 'weak' case, which will be used to determine the employee's entitlement to medical treatment and level of compensation (Ibid.: 43–5). The process, simply put, is arduously long. Proving emotional distress or depression as caused by work-related stress from bullying and or power harassment would hence be much more difficult.

It is no surprise that many victims of *ijime* and *pawahara* would rather suffer in silence than report their experiences to the authorities. As many of my informants explained, the burden of proof that is placed on them is unbearably heavy, like that of rape victims who are often required to prove that they had not behaved or were not dressed in a seductive manner to induce the rapist to commit the act of violence against them. The tendency of dismissing articles of workplace bullying and power harassment as trivial or non-existent could be worse when both the perpetrator and the victim are members of the weaker sex – that is, they are both female – whose behaviour is judged in terms of culturally constructed notions of gender. Among the several women I interviewed who had such experiences are Aoki Arisa and Tamura Tsuru.

Typical women's problems

Aoki was first introduced to Tamura by a mutual friend. The 36-year-old divorced single mother had just ended her marriage of eight years then and needed a better job than the part-time work she was doing. The 51-year-old Tamura, who was Senior Logistics and Billings Manager in a trading company, had searched with difficulty to fill the vacancy left by a subordinate who had recently resigned. After two rounds of formal interviews, Aoki was offered a full-time but two-year contractual position as Supervisor. Given that Aoki had been a good worker, Tamura later negotiated successfully for her subordinate to become a permanent employee with full benefits as Assistant Manager. Aoki worked harder than usual to show her appreciation to Tamura for being a supportive boss and mentor, and also to prove that she had earned the promotion based on her capabilities. They continued to work well for several years, until a corporate restructuring required the company's employee pool to be reduced by 20 per cent. Aoki also remained unscathed by the restructuring, and kept her position.

Tamura had not imagined herself to be targeted for redundancy. She had been with the company for nearly two decades, and had earned her superiors' trust in and recognition of her abilities. She had worked long hours – in the office and at home, on weeknights and weekends – for too many years that she could not remember when she had a good night's sleep. Tamura had also lost the entitlement to claim overtime compensation since becoming Assistant Manager, but increased her own out-of-pocket expenses on drinking with her team. Her team and many others had been working increasingly longer hours as staff turnover and staff shortage intensified following several rounds of corporate restructuring. Since it was company policy that employees at supervisory and managerial ranks could take time off in lieu of approved overtime work, Tamura began claiming one or two days off occasionally. However, she only had her superior's verbal approval, as he did not want too many employees to do the same. He had suggested that Tamura has Aoki cover for her. Should anyone ask, Aoki was to say that Tamura had some urgent family or personal matters to attend to.

One day, Aoki was told to split her job and spend half of her time in the Global Supply Chain division under another female manager Masuda Mieko. Her workload nearly doubled, though her salary remained little changed. Aoki had little choice but to work hard and hope the situation would improve. Her second boss treated her well too, entrusting Aoki with challenging but interesting tasks that made her better in managing difficult, higher-level work. However, Masuda also had a verbally agreed arrangement with her own boss, as Tamura did with hers. The mother of two would take several hours off work every fortnight for reasons she did not disclose to Aoki, who was to say that her boss was meeting a client outside the office if someone was to ask for Masuda's whereabouts. Aoki had realized by then that it was a common practice among members of the high-level management in the company to have such an implicit arrangement. Though the company allowed time off in lieu of overtime, to make an official claim would leave records of the number of overtime hours the employees in each division had worked. Those with excessively high overtime records could raise questions about the division's efficiency, which could affect employees' promotion prospects and their year-end bonus. That was the reason why the workers were often instructed to understate the overtime hours worked, which was also aimed at keeping each division's staff cost under control. Aoki could claim overtime pay and often had to work till midnight, but both her female bosses had instructed her to report less than half of her overtime hours. Exhausted from the double workload and long hours in the office, she had taken one or two days of sick leave, and was later cautioned by co-workers. Someone who had taken sick leave above the average number of days claimed by all the employees – regardless of the statutory annual sick leave one was entitled to – might be deemed as unproductive or unfit for work, and this could adversely affect the worker's annual performance review. Likewise, she heard that employees would also not claim all their annual leaves, for fear of receiving a poor appraisal due to perceptions of their being lazy or uncommitted to their job. Aoki was aware of arbitrary practices in corporations, and had personally encountered difficulties over her maternity leave at a previous workplace, but she was profoundly disturbed by the huge gaps in this company between the actual practices of employees, and the entitlements provided in the company policy and statutory laws.

After several months of working with Masuda, Aoki became aware that her second boss had been vying for Tamura's position for a long time, and had her several requests to replace Tamura's position rejected. Despite trying to keep conversations with both on work-related matters, working for two rival bosses became incrementally difficult for Aoki. Masuda would constantly ask Aoki about Tamura's work and schedule, as though she was looking for something negative about her rival. Tamura, however, had grown to trust her less since Aoki became a 'shared employee.' She would chide Aoki for making small mistakes, have Aoki work long hours to re-do tasks, and remind the subordinate that she was Aoki's main boss. As Masuda continued to be impressed by Aoki's capabilities, she later proposed that the latter become a full member of her team. Aoki suspected that this could be a ploy to weaken Tamura's position by taking one employer away. But the split arrangement had been exhausting. Aoki had by then been with the company for several years, and would like a promotion or at least a raise, to meet her child's costly educational expenses. Since Tamura had not been as supportive as she was in the past, Aoki decided to apply for a full transfer to Masuda's team that had infuriated Tamura, who refused to speak to Aoki unless it was unavoidable, when they had to discuss work.

Everything went well after joining Masuda's division until Aoki was summoned to a meeting with eight senior colleagues from Human Resource, Internal Audit, Compliance, and the Legal teams. Tamura's male boss and Masuda's superior were also present. She was told that both Tamura and Masuda had violated the company's policy by claiming many months' leave without approval, and asked to confirm this. Her two female superiors' male bosses denied any knowledge of the women's leave. Aoki was thus confused, and unsure about what she could or should say. She had recently heard rumours circulating in the office about an impending job cut. Were both Tamura and Masuda to be laid off, or was she the one, and many other questions were circling in Aoki's head, and she was afraid. The head of human resource was rather intimidating. He demanded to know what Aoki knew, while also warning her that she too would be violating the company policy for not reporting any misconduct or inappropriate behaviour that she was aware of. Both Tamura and Masuda had been good to her, and she would like to fend for them, but Aoki could not lie, as many co-workers knew of the two women's absences. Aoki explained cautiously that Tamura and Masuda had each informed her of absence on a few occasions due to work-related matters outside the office, though she did not know the specific details on what these matters were, whom they met, or where they went. Aoki was later made to repeat this several times at the meeting.

Tamura came by Aoki's desk the next day, called her a *uragimono* (traitor), and then walked out of the office. Tamura has been fired. Masuda's turn came the following day, but she left without speaking to Aoki. The official reason for the two women's dismissals was not announced till later in the week. Tamura and Masuda were said to have abused their position of power by compelling their subordinates to violate many of the company's policies, such as under-reporting overtime hours, making false claims of leave, and lying for them when they cheated the company by using office hours for personal activities. Aoki was more confounded by the unofficial version that the human resource manager had spread around the office. He had attributed the dismissals to 'typical women's problems' of not knowing how to act professionally, behaving in the office like housewives, and prioritizing their family interests over and above their work. The subsequent months were particularly difficult for Aoki, as word spread in the office that she had betrayed both her bosses, causing many co-workers to alienate her. Aoki resigned on her own accord half a year later to join a small private hospital, where she still works as consultant on pre-surgery procedures. She seemed quite relaxed when I met her in early 2019, which she said was due to a change in her attitude towards working:

> I do not enjoy my work as much as I did before. But it is good enough for me. I try to not pay attention to all the arbitrary and confusing things that are happening around me. I just hope I will not be bothered by them again. I am tired of being used, abused, and bullied. I do not want to work too hard any more for a promotion. It is not worth it. I am too tired. I work long hours in the office, and my work at home never ends.

> I only want a little satisfaction from what I do, pay the bills, go for a short holiday with my child once a year, and live a simple life.
>
> Ahh…but it is quite difficult to live a simple life in Japan nowadays, no? (*laughs*) You could be doing something bad and not get caught for as long as someone has your back. You can still be accused of a wrongdoing even if you have done everything right.

I had dinner with Tamura a week later, though I did not mention to her that I had met Aoki earlier. She said she was doing well as Business Development Manager in a multinational shipping and logistics corporation. She talked about what happened at her former workplace rather calmly, explaining that she knew the day would come when she would have to be a scapegoat for the company to justify a cost-cutting exercise, or a reduction in headcount. Those in middle management, especially women and older employees, are ‘popular targets’ for many companies. Women are dispensable anyway, and older ones are – like men – less productive and more expensive. The arrangement that she had made with her superior over the time off in lieu of overtime was only one among many practices among members of the upper management in the company. Having worked for numerous companies, Tamura knows that the obsession with performance statistics and measurements for maintaining a good corporate profile is the same everywhere across Japan. This obsession will only intensify, and not dissipate. This means that some employees will always be used as scapegoats, just like she and Masuda have been replaced by younger and cheaper new hires. She had not done anything wrong. She was just unlucky to be singled out at a time when she fitted the criteria for dismissal. There is little she could do to avoid being targeted again, and she explained why

> *Pawahara* is everywhere. It is a convenient tool for people with authority to use against you. So what if there are laws and policies? In Japan, the government and companies are a perfectly married couple. Yes, government laws are to be complied with, and companies can comply in so many different ways. It is the same with company policies, though they are mainly for show. Since the upper management set these policies, of course they know how to use them to their advantage.
>
> What can you do when you are at the bottom of the organization, a woman, someone old, or an old woman? You will always be the targets of *ijime*, *pawahara*, and abuse. When people in the upper management want to do something, they will find a way around a policy or even take advantage of one to suit their needs. They control the rules of the game, and you are the tools and targets in their game. The game never ends.

The game indeed goes on. Many cases of *pawahara* such as those having to enact gender roles, go out drinking, suffer nominal management, but what courses of action could they take to avoid these, or seek redress? Sano’s situation showed how helpless and precarious white-collar workers are.

As the women managers' experiences described earlier show, workplace bullying and power harassment are far more varied than the examples given in the six categories listed by MHLW. They are also more complex, and intertwined with deep-seated cultural values and practices, especially those relating to gender. Compiling an exhaustive list and clarifying definitions would still be insufficient to prevent or minimize acts of *ijime* and *pawahara* without a proper system of monitoring and stringent penalties. More importantly, the country's judiciary would also need to define or recognize workplace bullying and power harassment as an actionable tortious act (Hsiao 2015: 188). Until then, the new legislation would be yet another ineffective item for display that perhaps projects the Japanese government as having made an attempt to curb the proliferating workplace problems, just as the EEOL has been since its implementation in 1986. However, unlike the EEOL, the new law is likely to be counter-effective and could potentially exacerbate the diverse difficulties that employees are already encountering, as the cases detailed earlier have demonstrated. Without the support of strong labour unions in the country, Japanese workers – both male and female – would have to brace themselves for a darker, bleaker, and tumultuous work environment in the future.

Notes

1 The ten-episode weekly drama was first broadcast by TV Tokyo on 15 October 2018 at the 22:00 hours primetime slot.

2 *Aru* is an abbreviation of the romanization of the English word 'alcohol.' *Aruhara* is not new, and is widely known in Japan as referring to someone who has been pressured or compelled to go out drinking with co-workers or superiors.

3 The Japanese word *gyaku* means 'reverse.' The drama explains *gyakuhara* as a situation when a person in a superior position in the office has his or her position of superiority undermined by a subordinate, who may refuse to take instructions from the superior, or perform tasks that defy the superior's orders.

4 The word *pata* is an abbreviation of 'paternity.' As discussed in Chapter 3, Japanese men are entitled to paternity leave, but may be pressured into taking some or none at all. One episode of the drama delves into how this would constitute as a form of harassment.

5 *Risu* is abbreviated from the English word 'restructuring.' In the drama, an employee could be said to experience *risuhara* when he or she is forced to accept a transfer to an inferior position or to a branch office far away from his or her current place of work, in the hope that the employee would eventually resign, and hence save the company on paying any compensation.

6 This is a combination of the Japanese word *sewa* – which means 'care' – and the shortened English word for 'harassment,' to refer to verbal abuse or behaviour that would cause someone to experience discomfort, embarrassment, or shame.

7 This legislation was revised in 2017 in response to pressures from the public to allow workers bearing responsibilities of providing childcare and nursing care to obtain leave. One revision, for example, allows a worker to take nursing care leave of up to 93 days in three separate increments, and not all at once.

8 A tort under common law jurisdictions is a civil act that wrongfully infringes on the right (outside a contract) of a person that causes the person to suffer harm or loss for which the party who commits the act could be held legally liable to pay a compensation.

6 A shiny or more precarious future?

Hashimoto Seiko became the second woman to join Prime Minister Abe Shinzo's Cabinet which was reshuffled on 11 September 2019. However, her new position is that of Minister in charge of the 2020 Tokyo Olympics and Paralympics. This change for the former lawmaker in the House of Councillors – the upper house of the National Diet – pales in contrast to the headline-grabbing appointment of Koizumi Shinjiro, son of former Prime Minister Koizumi Junichiro (2001–2006), as Environment Minister. Adding Hashimoto, a former speed skater, to a contingent role in the Cabinet with limited portfolio, and ahead of the summer games in 2020, evidently showed a lack of genuine efforts by Abe's government to make Japanese women 'shine' with the highly marketed policy on womenomics. This came as no surprise to many in Japan, especially the subjects of this book. In fact, the state's agenda on womenomics looks set to intensify the treatment of women as a contingent workforce and expendable resource for the economy. Given the range of difficulties that female corporate managers have experienced, the future could hardly be deemed a bright one.

No doubt, more women in Japan would benefit from new opportunities for them to pursue professional careers and even advance higher up the corporate ladder, as many have in recent decades. And more would also be able to enhance their economic position, develop life trajectories outside the realm of domesticity, and re-conceptualize gender identities based on salaried work. Yet, further challenges also await them, especially given the range of structural difficulties that still exist to present conflicts in their lives, and exacerbate the precarious conditions that many women are already caught in. With persistently unchanging cultural perceptions of gender and arbitrary labour laws, coupled with a lack of union support for collective bargaining, what might the future be like for young women in the white-collar workforce today who aspire to become the future generations of corporate managers? Perhaps the accounts of a young management trainee's experience might provide a glimpse of the future of womenomics.

I first met Hayami Hikari when her mother Hayami Hikari brought the 11-year-old for a weekend stroll with me. I have since watched the little girl grow into an intelligent, mature, and sensible 26-year-old filled with aspirations, determination, optimism, and pragmatism. I arranged to meet Hikari[1] for dinner at seven one Friday evening during my Tokyo visit in June 2019, though the young management trainee could not arrive till a quarter to nine. She apologized profusely upon arrival at the restaurant, despite having done so in the numerous text messages that she had sent from the office. She was supposed to have finished an important project, and was certain she could leave the office earlier than usual. But something had come up, as always. Hikari has worked in a large Japanese advertising company for nearly three years. Is that why she looks pale and gaunt in the grey pantsuit and white shirt she was wearing that evening? Yes, she has not had enough sleep since joining the company, nor taken her meals regularly. The work hours are long, and work often spills into the weekends. She misses playing tennis and going out with her friends, as she used to do before graduating from university. Most of all, she misses her boyfriend whom she would meet twice or thrice a week briefly after work. He is also a busy management trainee in a Japanese bank, where he would often work overnight.

The young couple plans to get married a few years later, when they are both more settled in their respective jobs. As management trainees, they are each required to work for a short duration of time in one division and move to various others until they are given a more permanent position. The work day is long, and the hours erratic. The couple would like to have children and lead a reasonably comfortable lifestyle, and must, therefore, work hard and maintain two sources of income. They could not afford to live on one income, and neither Hikari nor her boyfriend would want her to stop working and be a *sengyō shufu* (full-time housewife). To this young generation of Japanese, work is as much about self-fulfilment as it is about economic independence. But the young couple is already feeling burnt out after working for only few years.

For Hikari, the exhaustion and stress from long hours of work are slightly more bearable than the frustrations of working in an environment where the mixing of old and new cultural values collides with conflicts produced by a fusion of Japanese and global work practices. She describes her office as an *okashī senjō* (strange or comical battlefield) where junior employees are trained to fight a war with a constantly changing armoury of modern and ancient weapons issued by the company. Yet, Hikari quite likes her job despite the heavy workload. She has many opportunities to work with colleagues from different countries and diverse cultural backgrounds. The ability to exchange ideas and apply a variety of approaches to a given assignment is exciting and thrilling. Her employer would constantly roll out new slogans and mottos that emulate those of American and European multinational corporations for the purpose of motivating employees, and making them believe that they are working for a modern international firm. Yet, the company still preserves many old Japanese practices, and is fairly resistant to change. Junior employees are encouraged to express themselves freely, and are required to submit reports on a regular basis to propose new, innovative ideas for expanding the firm's business. But these proposals are rarely accepted by the company's board of directors, which comprises a total of 15 men aged above 60 years. Hikari finds this exercise futile and exhausting, but not doing so would reflect badly on junior employees whose performance reviews and promotion prospects could be severely compromised.

Bullying and harassment as legitimate in modern business

This regular assignment reminds Hikari of the countless exercises she used to do in school, when she had to write an essay regularly on how she would like to change the cultural environment in Japan, improve the lives of people in their local communities, transform Japanese society, and contribute to their country's economy. Is this what corporate managers do, that is, endlessly performing futile tasks, she often wonders. Could this be considered as a form of *ijime* or *pawahara*, she has asked her mother and boyfriend. Hikari and other junior employees in the company have also raised these questions. No, the exercises they do are not futile, and you are not being bullied into doing these assignments, a senior employee has responded at a training seminar. These are important assignments that are necessary for their job in advertising. They should not entertain the thought of bullying or harassment. It would amount to professional suicide, that is, the legal team would bring the full force of the company to crush a complaint or legal suit on such a matter. Hikari could not stop laughing as she imitated the trainer's stern look and deep voice.

Indeed, the company is a massive organization with considerable financial resources, and its compliance and legal teams will ensure that everything it does is in accordance to the law. A new harassment counselling team was formed recently to provide consultations and accept complaints relating to *ijime* and *pawahara*, and the new staff compliance handbook contains several hundred pages of rules and regulations for all employees to observe. Employees are required to attend regular training programmes to familiarize themselves with the rules and regulations. The company has everything in place that is needed to be a law-abiding and respectable organization with high standards of professional ethics. The firm is, thus, flawless and faultless, at least on paper. The reality, however, is quite different.

'Work comes first' is a phrase that Hikari and all her co-workers are frequently reminded to uphold. On paper, the company offers extensive medical leave, annual holiday, and overtime compensation, as well as leisure activities for employees to enjoy a good work-life balance. The staff manual stipulates very clearly the maximum overtime hours that each team could work, and recommends various activities provided by the company for employees to relieve stress. In reality, few employees would dare clock overtime beyond the number of hours set arbitrarily by their respective division heads or project leaders. Even fewer workers would take a day off sick, especially when their team is rushing to meet the deadline for an important project.

Hikari and other female junior employees are at times treated a little more leniently, since women are perceived as 'the weaker sex' who cannot withstand the pressure and long hours as well as their male co-workers. A few project leads, however, seem to think differently and believe that 'the weaker sex' requires more severe training in order to build their level of endurance. Hikari has to carefully adjust her behaviour when working under different superiors. She has taken non-drowsy medication for her cold, and pretended to be well while she worked continuously alongside her team members. On two occasions, she was granted a half day of sick leave by a reasonably kind superior, though she had to work from home while resting in bed.

How does one draw the boundary between doing what is a necessary part of one's job, and being bullied to do more than what is required for one's job? How could a junior employee such as herself be heard properly when traditional forms of bullying and harassment are now dressed in the modern business garb of professional excellence and are therefore legitimate? How might the company's compliance counselling centre respond to Hikari's complaint about some of the happenings? More importantly, would she be alienated by other project leaders once it has become known that she has reported on a superior's unruly or unfair treatment of subordinates? As one trainee has said, it would be professional suicide. Hikari laughed as she described the compliance office as a minefield to deter employees from filing complaints, and added that what is unreported, therefore, does not exist.

Management-track as an endless trail leading to a dead-end

What Hikari also realizes is that the so-called management-track career for trainees is a 'never-ending, obscure road' that abruptly takes one to an *ikidomari* (dead-end). On seeing my puzzled look, the young woman quickly explains that the management-track is a *dokonimo tsugaranai nagai michi* (long trail that leads nowhere) for women, and so the opportunity to be a part of the company's management *gensō tekina mokuhyō* (an elusive goal). The company hires some 30 fresh undergraduates every year as management trainees to provide a steady stream of cheap, hardworking workers to do all the lowest-level tasks. Moving the management trainees from one division to another periodically ensures that every team gets to benefit from this pool of economical labour to keep their operating costs low. Since the cost of keeping a third-year trainee is higher than that of a new trainee's, the company will let the majority of them go, and hire another batch of fresh undergraduates. Only a handful of management trainees from each batch will be selected to join a division or team after the third year, though most will be offered a short-term contract with a duration of three to five years. In short, a management trainee is a temporary worker on a three-year contract, which may be extended for another short duration. The title 'management' is thus meaningless.

Hikari is now close to the end of her third year, and has been thinking a lot about whether her contract would be extended. She has also thought about the prospects for *kyaria appu* (career advancement) within the company in the longer term. The top two levels of management are male, while the 20-member third layer of management comprises several non-executive female officers who are representatives from outside the company. No woman has lasted for more than ten years with the advertising agency, which has more than two thousand employees. The few who did have reached only the highest level of the middle management. While this is the 'dead-end' for female employees on management-track hoping to *kyaria appu*, the struggle to reach there is also an arduously long and difficult one. There is fierce competition among the female employees, as their work performances are evaluated more harshly than their male counterparts. Still, Hikari would like to try out that path, if only she could have the opportunity. She graduated from one of the top universities in Japan with distinctions in Business and Economics. Surely, this must count for something.

At the same time, she also doubts if she has the energy to persist. As a management trainee, Hikari has to plan projects, write business reports, produce market analyses, manage interns, perform evaluations of her peers' work, assess her own performance, gather information about new developments in the operations of her employer's rivals, collate statistics on competitors' efficiency, benchmark the productivity of her division's work against others, and assist in prospecting for new clients. In addition to attending training programmes, she also has to frequently run errands for various superiors that are unrelated to work. A tiny slip would cost her a bad performance review, which will, in turn, disrupt the progress in her transfer to another division, and also delay her promotion. Despite having performed poorly on one project, Hikari was twice 'upgraded' all because more women were needed to re-calibrate the gender profile of a division. She has been told that this strategy is usually employed when the financial reporting season approaches, mainly to impress shareholders, potential investors, and regulators. Given the limited opportunities for female employees to develop a sense of *ibasho* (belonging) or find a meaningful purpose for their hard work in such a corporate environment, Hikari can hardly foresee a medium-term career – let alone a long-term one – as a manager in the company.

Drinking with co-workers as choice and coercion

The 26-year-old has not told Hayami much about what goes on in her workplace, though her mother is aware of the pressure she is under. Hikari has collapsed in bed in her work clothes many times. She has also talked about work in her sleep. Hayami has been worried ever since her daughter received the job offer from the company. Her biggest fear is that Hikari might suffer a similar fate as that of many young workers: *karōshi* (death from overwork). Hayami has been particularly disturbed by news reports on the suicide of the 24-year-old woman in 2015 due to excessive overwork while employed by Japan's largest advertising agency Dentsu. That is not all. Another of Hayami's fear is that her daughter might fall ill or die from excessive drinking.

Judging from the young woman's alcohol intake that evening in 2019, it was apparent to me that Hikari is no longer the teenager I once knew who used to fall asleep after two glasses of beer. 'I have had a lot of practice,' she laughed. She would not be able to do well in marketing and advertising if she could not drink. Regular drinking among workers is highly encouraged by her employer, as it is good for team-building, though at employees' own individual expense. Drinking with clients is a must, and usually in the company of senior employees who are mostly male. The boundary between choice and coercion is fluid, shifting, and at times overlapping. If Hikari could help it, she would obviously rather spend a quiet evening with her boyfriend, or slouch in front of the television at home. But she does not wish to be the only one absent from a drinking session. It would reflect badly on her as a non-team player. And when her co-workers are drinking alcoholic beverages, Hikari could not insist on a soft drink or tea. How could her participation in social drinking with co-workers be regarded as a form of *aruhara* (alcohol harassment) when no one overtly compels her to go out drinking with her co-workers, to consume alcohol, or to drink plenty of it? Could she blame anyone if she was to become an alcoholic or fall ill due to excessive drinking?

Unchanging social perceptions of gender

There are many issues that confuse and puzzle Hikari as she struggles to make sense of the activities in her workplace. One thing that seems clear to her, though, is that attitudes towards women are distinctly fossilized in time. Working in advertising allows her to understand the active role by this industry in contributing to creating and propagating gendered discourses and representations. Two-thirds of each batch of management trainees are male, along with 75 per cent of the company's employees. Women are mostly at the lower strata of the corporate structure, and strategically placed in every division as props for enhancing the company's image. The company is run by men for men. Sexist jokes could be heard every day in the office. Work tasks performed by female employees are often described and dismissed as *onna no shigoto* (women's job). When a female worker makes a mistake or could not do a job well, a comment that is commonly made is *onna dakara* (because she is female). In addition to gender discrimination, derogatory remarks on age, ethnicity, and religion are also made by many, and legitimized as necessary for brainstorming and intellectual discussions that are important to the company's business.

All the efforts that have gone into compiling the compliance handbook and conducting training programmes for employees to cultivate better treatment of one another and curb practices of *ijime* and *pawahara* do not seem to have effected any improvement. Perhaps there was such an intention to begin with, just like the contradiction between the daily practice of 'Work Comes First' in the office, and the company's stated motto 'People First.' In fact, there is no contradiction at all. They are meant for two separate categories of people. The former applies to employees, while the latter is for customers, who are to be treated with understanding and great care since they are individuals with real lives, varied attitudes, and diverse needs that require special attention. Hikari hence draws the conclusion that few people in Japan are willing to change many habits, values, attitudes, and practices that they have been accustomed to for many years. As a member of the 'weaker sex,' she must learn to deal with any conflict in her identity and many other issues that are considered to be 'women's problems.'

Hikari's hope for improvements to women's status in Japan waned further after the recent change in the country's imperial succession. Despite popular polls in support of a woman to ascend the throne, and despite also efforts by former Prime Minister Koizumi Junichiro to review the Imperial Household Law that was implemented during the Meiji era in 1889, no revision was made by Abe's cabinet to permit the reign of the country by a female monarch.[2] An amendment was made to the antiquated law to allow Emperor Akihito to be the first Japanese monarch to abdicate the throne in 200 years, ending his 30-year reign as Emperor Heisei.[3] However, no change was made to permit the enthronement of Crown Prince Naruhito as the new Emperor Reiwa[4] be witnessed by his wife, the new Empress Masako, or their only child Princess Aiko. The private ceremony was attended by male officials, with the exception of Katayama Satsuki, who was the sole female member of Abe's Cabinet at that time. Hikari has this to say:

> Abe is not sincere at all in making any real change to Japanese society or improving gender equality. Not allowing Princess Aiko to take over from her father in the future, and not allowing Princess Masako to attend the enthronement of the new Emperor, only made it clear how backward Japan is when compared to Europe, and even China and South Korea (*sighs*). Women in this country still have a very long and difficult battle to fight…

What is the future of womenomics?

It is interesting, and also rather disturbing, to note the frequent allusion to war in the narratives of a young woman of Hikari's age. She has started working not so long so, and yet has experienced various struggles that would probably persist through her working life. Perhaps the war references point to her realization of the tenuous journey that she has to brace herself for. Or, perhaps women of her generation grew up playing video and computer games filled with war themes that she has used war references out of habit. While the 26-year-old shows incredible maturity and has an acute awareness of her social environment, it remains to be seen as to whether she is able to manage more conflicts and contradictions that may present themselves in the years to come. In the gaming world, there are clearly defined rules, set weapons, specific targets, and recommended strategies to fight and win a battle. Reality, however, requires individuals to learn from experience and develop ample flexibility to adapt to changing circumstances and situations. For many young informants of Hikari's age, they share the common difficulty of managing a stable and coherent self-identity. This is shaped not only by how the women have been trained to perceive themselves and how they are being perceived by others, but also by how these women manage the changes to their self-perceptions over time to achieve a meaningful sense of who they are as individuals, and not as mere gendered beings in Japanese society (Ho 2018: 194–5).

The young generation of today is 'soft' because they have been educated differently from the previous generations. Born and bred in the neoliberal era, Hikari and young Japanese have been trained to embrace the various neoliberal ideals of individual freedom and self-responsibility, which oblige them to respond to the duty call to pursue self-discovery and self-fulfilment (Cave 2001: 177; Dore and Sako 1998: 111; Matsunaga 2000: 44). Yet, the possibility of attaining all these through work is limited, if not worsening (Brinton 2011; Genda 2005). The disjuncture between their ideals and social reality is hence far greater for young women than it was for women of previous generations whose experiences are those of the disjuncture between prevailing gender role expectations of women and offers of financial independence by broader economic change.

Hikari may indeed be right to describe her current situation to a battlefield. As women continue to be valued for their contributions as a resource for the broader economy and not as individuals, they are caught in the conflict zone where their desire and need to recognize themselves as individuals with potential in society are ignored, while they are appreciated as mere tools to be mobilized for the economic benefits of others. Their future is thus a problematic and precarious one with serious long-term implications on gender dynamics, family formations, and social relations in Japan. More significantly, ignoring the stability of socio-cultural developments in favour of economic goals could lead to burgeoning social problems and destabilization of cultural values that may generate heavy longer-term socio-economic costs to the economy (Allison 2013; Slater 2011). Womenomics could work effectively and meaningfully, but only when women are appreciated as valuable resource and given thoughtful nurturing and proper care. The following words by Hikari might otherwise portend what the future of Japan would be like:

> I am not sure if my future would be brighter than what my mother had when she was my age. I would like to be optimistic, but the view ahead is unclear, and at times rather gloomy. Everyone says that women have the same difficulties as men in today's work environment, and women are given similar opportunities as men. Sure, surviving the workplace is not easy for anyone, male or female. But women are still treated as inferiors, and so what are our chances of surviving or succeeding?
>
> I will continue to hope, but I am not very sure what I am hoping for. For the government to be more serious about managing its laws? For companies to exploit workers less? For Japanese people to improve on

> their attitudes towards and treatment of women? If there is insufficient changes happening soon, then Japan will soon be full of workers who are physically ill, emotionally depressed, mentally disturbed, and probably also socially destructive. I could only say good luck to those who wish to manage an economy that is full of such people…

It is a pity to hear a young woman of her age expressing such a bleak view of her future. She is well-educated, optimistic, and hardworking, despite belonging to what is widely known as a soft generation. The hopes and aspirations of young women – and men – like Hikari would be quickly vanquished should the structural conditions in Japan continue to be resistant to change to incorporate the needs and manage the demands of the country's future workforce.

To be nipped while budding, young women's battle would be lost at the outset. Perhaps Abe's womenomics would indeed be a curse on women, with its claim to make women 'shine' intended as a pun that also commands women 'to die' (*shine*). If this was the case, the price to pay for another despondent generation by Japanese society and the country's economy would be incalculably high.

A study of this nature risks being misinterpreted as offering biased accounts of corporate managers in Japan that cast women only as victims in a structurally inhibitive system. It also risks being misunderstood for dismissing the difficulties that Japanese men too encounter as managers. It is not within the scope of this research to include detailed discussions on the precarious experiences of male managers, though it is hoped that this study has paved the way for further studies on the extent to which the neoliberal transformations of work in today's flexible work environment are adversely affecting the sustainability of the socio-economic lives of workers in various professions and occupational statuses.

Notes

1 As explained in Chapter 1, I refer to the younger Hayami by her first name Hikari to avoid any confusion.
2 Since the current law forbids women from succeeding the imperial throne, Prince Akishino – son of Prince Hisahito, the new Emperor Reiwa's brother – is next in line to the succession, and not the Emperor Reiwa's only child Princess Aiko.
3 Emperor Akihito abdicated the throne on 30 April 2019, ending the reign Heisei (peace everywhere) which began on 8 January 1989, a day following the death of Emperor Hirohito whose reign was known as Showa, which means 'enlightened peace.'
4 The new reign Reiwa, which means 'beautiful harmony,' officially began on 1 May 2019.

Appendix

Profiles of subjects (*arranged in order of appearance in this book*)

Order	*Chapter*	*Name*	*Sex*	*Age (2019)*	*Marital status*	*Children*	*No of jobs since graduation*		*Education*	*Current job title*	*Current employer*	*Company size*
							Total	*Regular jobs*				
1	**1**	HAYAMI Harue	F	51	Divorced	1	7	4	BA in Economics and Finance; Diploma in Banking	Senior Economist	Foreign	Medium
2	**1**	HAYAMI Hikari	F	26	Single	0	1	1	BA in Business and Economics	Senior Management Trainee	Japanese	Large
3	**1**	NAKAO Nyoko	F	53	Divorced	1	4	2	BA in Law; MA in International Finance	Legal Director	Foreign	Medium
4	**1**	NAKAO Niki	F	27	Single	0	3	1	BA in Global Hospitality Management	Trainee Chef	Japanese	Small
5	**2**	KISHIDA Kiyoko	F	46	Single	0	6	3	BA in English Literature and Philosophy	Deputy Head of Corporate Communications	Foreign	Medium
6	**2**	SAWABE Sayori	F	45	Divorced	1	5	4	BA in Business and Marketing; Diploma in Purchasing	Manager of Merchandising	Foreign	Medium
7	**2**	NAMIKI Naomi	F	45	Married	0	8	5	BA in Law and Business Studies	Business Development Manager	Japanese	Medium
8	**2**	TAKAGI Tomoe	F	39	Single	0	6	6	BA in Business and Marketing; Diploma in Communications	Public Relations Manager	Japanese	Medium
9	**2**	MEMOTO Mio	F	49	Single (co-habiting with same partner for 25 years)	0	9	5	BA in Finance; MBA; Diplomas in Taxation and Financial Analysis	Financial Controller	Foreign	Medium

(*Continued*)

Order	*Chapter*	*Name*	*Sex*	*Age (2019)*	*Marital status*	*Children*	*No of jobs since graduation*		*Education*	*Current job title*	*Current employer*	*Company size*
							Total	*Regular jobs*				
10	**2**	SOMA Seiko	F	48	Single	0	11	7	BA in Business Administration; MBA; CFA	Treasury Manager	Foreign	Large
11	**2**	HIRAI Hanako	F	52	Married	0	12	7	BA in Finance and Business Studies; CPA	Senior Finance Manager	Japanese	Small
12	**2**	IWAKI Ikue	F	46	Divorced	0	4	3	High School Certificate; Diploma in Human Resource Management	Senior Manager of Human Resource	Japanese	Medium
13	**2**	FUKUDA Fumiko	F	43	Divorced	1	6	4	BSc in Engineering; MSc in Transport Communications	Logistics and Billing Manager	Foreign	Small
14	**3**	SASAKI Shiori	F	51	Divorced	0	6	5	BA in Linguistics; Diploma in Finance and Taxation; CPA	Manager of Customer Support	Foreign	Medium
15	**3**	KIZAKI Kazumi	F	46	Married	2	5	4	BA in International Studies; Diploma in Human Resource Management	Human Resource Director	Foreign	Small
16	**3**	MIURA Miho	F	46	Married	0	4	4	International Baccalaureate in European History; Diploma in Business Studies	Senior Marketing Consultant	Foreign	Medium
17	**3**	KIMURA Kotaro	M	48	Single	0	3	3	BA in Asian Studies and Business Management	Sales Supervisor	Foreign	Small
18	**3**	TANAKA Takeo	M	46	Married	1	4	4	BA in Strategic Management	Senior Business Development Manager	Japanese	Medium
19	**3**	GOHARA Kozue	F	52	Married	2	7	6	BA in Finance; Diploma in Taxation	Finance Manager	Japanese	Medium

20	**3**	YAMADA Yasuo	M	36	Married	1	4	3	High School Certificate; Diploma in Business and Accounting	Accounting Supervisor	Japanese	Medium
21	**3**	UMEDA Yoriko	F	48	Single	0	4	4	BA in Management Studies; Diploma in Marketing	Sales and Marketing Director	Japanese	Medium
22	**3**	OHNO Rena	F	44	Single (co-habiting with same partner for more than 6 years)	0	6	3	BA in Global Management and Economics; Diploma in International Banking	Vice President of Regional Development	Japanese	Large
23	**4**	ARAI Ayumi	F	38	Married	0	4	3	BA in Law and Finance	Legal Team Leader	Japanese	Small
24	**4**	ISHIDA Izumi	F	46	Married	1	5	3	BSc in Computing; Diploma in Business and Finance	Special Project Team Manager	Japanese	Small
25	**4**	ENDO Eriko	F	43	Married	1	5	2	BA in China Studies and Marketing; MBA	Senior Vice President of Regional Sales	Foreign	Medium
26	**4**	NUKAGA Nao	F	48	Single	0	5	4	BSc in Biology and Nutrition Studies; Diplomas in Finance and Taxation	Assistant Payroll Manager	Japanese	Small
27	**4**	KOJIMA Kaeko	F	43	Single	0	6	3	BA in Languages and Business Studies; Diploma in Marketing	Senior Business Development Manager	Foreign	Small
28	**4**	NOMOTO Natsue	F	47	Divorced	1	8	5	BA in Finance; MBA; CPA	Senior Finance Manager	Japanese	Medium
29	**5**	SANO Sayaka	F	48	Married	0	7	5	BSc in Economics; Certificates in Business Consultancy and Finance	Senior Management Consultant	Foreign	Medium

(*Continued*)

Order	*Chapter*	*Name*	*Sex*	*Age (2019)*	*Marital status*	*Children*	*No of jobs since graduation*		*Education*	*Current job title*	*Current employer*	*Company size*
							Total	*Regular jobs*				
30	**5**	OKADA Omi	F	44	Married	0	4	3	BA in International Relations; MA in Business Communications; Certificate in Marketing	Director of Corporate Communications	Foreign	Medium
31	**5**	MURATA Mayo	F	46	Single (co-habiting with same partner for 11 years)	0	6	4	BSc and MSc in Land Planning; Diploma in Corporate Communications	Customer Services and Relations Manager	Japanese	Large
32	**5**	AOKI Arisa	F	36	Divorced	1	7	3	High School Certificate; Diploma in Finance and Taxation	Business Consultant	Japanese	Small
33	**5**	TAMURA Tsuru	F	51	Divorced	0	6	4	BA in Philosophy and History; Diplomas in Finance and Taxation; CPA	Business Development Manager	Foreign	Large
34	**5**	MASUDA Mieko	F	48	Married	2	5	4	BA in Public Administration; Diploma in Business Management	Senior Manager of Business Planning	Foreign	Medium

References

Adelstein, Jake (2017) 'Japan Is Literally Working Itself to Death: How Can It Stop?'. *Forbes*, 30 October. Accessible online at: www.forbes.com/sites/adelsteinjake/2017/10/30/japan-is-literally-working-itself-to-death-how-can-it-stop/#c96ff282f144 [accessed 30 September 2019].

Alexy, Allison (2011) 'Intimate Dependence and Its Risks in Neoliberal Japan', *Anthropological Quarterly*, 84(4): 895–917.

Allison, Anne (1994) *Nightwork: Sexuality, Pleasure and Corporate Masculinity in a Tokyo Hostess Club*. Chicago and London: University of Chicago Press.

Allison, Anne (2012) 'Ordinary Refugees: Social Precarity and Soul in 21st Century Japan', *Anthropological Quarterly,* 85(2): 345–70.

Allison, Anne (2013) *Precarious Japan*. Durham and London: Duke University Press.

Atsumi, Reiko (1979) '*Tsukiai*: Obligatory Personal Relationships of Japanese White-Collar Employees', *Human Organization,* 38(1): 63–70.

Bando, Mariko (2006) *Josei no Hinkaku* [The Qualities of A Woman]. Tokyo: PHP Kenkyūjo.

BBC (2017) 'Dentsu's Overtime Fine Puts Spotlight on Japan's Work Culture'. *The British Broadcasting Corporation*, 6 October. Accessible online at: www.bbc.com/news/business-41521460 [accessed 30 September 2019].

Befu, Harumi (1986) 'An Ethnography of Dinner Entertainment in Japan', in Takie Sugiyama Lebra and William P. Lebra (eds.) *Japanese Culture and Behavior*, pp. 108–20. Honolulu: University of Hawai'i Press.

Ben-Ari, Eyal (2002) 'At the Interstices: Drinking, Management, and Temporary Groups in a Local Japanese Organization', in Joy Hendry and Massino Raveri (eds.) *Japan at Play: The Ludic and the Logic of Power*, pp. 129–51. London: Routledge.

Biehl, João (2016) 'The Postneoliberal Fabulation of Power: On Statecraft, Precarious Infrstructures, and Public Mobilization in Brazil', *American Ethnologist,* 43(3): 437–50.

Blind, Georg D., and Stefania Lottantivon Mandach (2015) 'Decades not Lost, but Won: Increased Employment, Higher Wages, and More Equal Opportunities in the Japanese Labour Market', *Social Science Japan Journal*, 18(1): 63–88.

Borovoy, Amy (2005) *The Too-Good-Wife: Alcohol, CoDependency, and the Politics of Nurturance in Postwar Japan*. Berkeley, Los Angeles and London: University of California Press.

Borovoy, Amy (2011) 'Japan as Mirror: Neoliberalism's Promise and Costs', in: Carol J. Greenhouse (ed.) *Ethnographies of Neoliberalism*, pp. 60–74. Philadelphia: University of Pennsylvania Press.

Bousquet, Marc (2002) 'The Waste Product of Graduate Education: Toward a Dictatorship of the Flexible', *Social Text,* 20(1): 80–104.

Brinton, Mary C. (1992) 'Christmas Cakes and Wedding Cakes: The Social Organization of Japanese Women's Life Course', in Takie Sugiyama Lebra (ed.) *Japanese Social Organization*, pp. 79–107. Honolulu: University of Hawai'i Press.

Brinton, Mary C. (1993) *Women and the Economic Miracle: Gender and Work in Postwar Japan.* Berkeley, Los Angeles and London: University of California Press.

Brinton, Mary C. (2011) *Lost in Transition: Youth, Work, and Instability in Postindustrial Japan.* Cambridge: Cambridge University Press.

Broadbent, Kaye (2010) ''For Women, By Women': Women-Only Unions in Japan', *Japan Forum,* 17(2): 213–30.

Campbell, Stephen (2016) 'Everyday Recomposition: Precarity and Socialization in Thailand's Migrant Workforce', *American Ethnologist,* 43(2): 258–69.

Cangià, Flavia (2018) 'Precarity, Imagination, and the Mobile Life of the 'Trailing Spouse'', *Ethos,* 46(1): 8–26.

Cave, Peter (2001) 'Educational Reform in Japan in the 1990s: 'Individuality' and Other Uncertainties', *Comparative Education,* 37(2): 173–91.

Chaplin, Sarah (2007) *Japanese Love Hotels: A Cultural History.* London and New York: Routledge.

Chauvière, Michel, and Stephen S. Mick (2011) 'The French Sociological Critique of Managerialism: Themes and Frameworks', *Critical Sociology,* 39(1): 135–43.

Chiba, Kaeko (2011) *Japanese Women, Class and the Tea Ceremony.* London and New York: Routledge.

Creighton, Millie R. (1996) 'Marriage, Motherhood and Career', in Anne Imamura (ed.) *Re-Imaging Japanese Women*, pp. 192–220. Berkeley: University of California Press.

Curtin, Michael, and Kevin Sanson, eds. (2016) *Precarious Creativity: Global Media, Local Labor.* Oakland: University of California Press.

De Certeau, Michel (1984) *The Practice of Everyday Life.* Berkeley, Los Angeles and New York: University of California Press.

De Gaulejac, Vincent (2009) *La société malade de la gestion. Idéologie gestionnaire, pouvoir managérial et harcèlement social* [Society's Management Sickness: Management Ideology, Managerial Power and Social Harassment]. Paris: Seuil.

De Gaulejac, Vincent (2011) *Travail, les raisons de la colère* [Work: The Reasons for Anger]. Paris: Seuil.

Dentsu (2018) *Information Media Trends in Japan 2018: Information Media White Paper.* Tokyo: Dentsu Media Innovation Lab.

Doi, Takeo (1971) *Amae no Kōzō* [Anatomy of Dependence]. Tokyo: Kōbundo.

Doi, Takeo (1973) *The Anatomy of Dependence.* Translated by John Bester. Tokyo, New York and London: Kodansha International.

Doi, Takeo (1986) *The Anatomy of Self: The Individual versus Society.* Tokyo, New York and London: Kodansha International.

Dore, Ronald (1973) *British Factory – Japanese Factory: The Origins of National Diversity in Industrial Relation.* London: George Allen and Unwin.

Dore, Ronald (2000) *Stock Market Capitalism: Welfare Capitalism: Japan and Germany versus the Anglo-Saxons.* Oxford: University of Oxford.

Dore, Ronald, and Mari Sako (1998) *How The Japanese Learn to Work.* London and New York: Routledge.

Edwards, Walter (1989) *Modern Japan through Its Weddings.* Stanford, California: Stanford University Press.

Ehrenberg, Alain (1991) *Le Culte de la Performance* [The Cult of Performance]. Paris: Hachette Littérature.

Ehrenreich, Barbara, and Arlie Russell Hochschild, eds. (2002) *Global Woman: Nannies, Maids, and Sex Workers in the New Economy.* London: Granta.

Ettlinger, Nancy (2007) 'Precarity Unbound', *Alternatives,* 32: 319–40.

Foucault, Michel (1991) 'Governmentality', in Colin Gordon Graham Burchell, and Peter Miller (eds.) *The Foucault Effect: Studies in Governmentality*, pp. 87–104. Chicago: University of Chicago Press.

Fujimura, Hiroyuki (2012) 'Japan's Labor Unions: Past, Present, Future', *Japan Labor Review,* 9(1): 6–24.

Fujimura-Fanselow, Kumiko, and Atsuko Kameda (1995) 'The Changing Portrait of Japanese Men', in Kumiko Fujimura-Fanselow and Atsuko Kameda (eds.) *Japanese Women: New Feminist Perspectives on the Past, Present, and Future*, pp. 229–30. New York: The Feminist Press.

Fujita, Mariko (1989) "It's All Mother's Fault': Childcare and the Socialization of Working Mothers in Japan', *Journal of Japanese Studies,* 15(1): 67–91.

Gagné, Nana Okura (2018) '"Correcting Capitalism": Changing Metrics and Meanings of Work among Japanese Employees', *Journal of Contemporary Asia*, 48(1): 67–87.

Gagné, Nana Okura (2019) 'Neoliberalism at Work: Corporate Reforms, Subjectivity, and Post- Toyotist Affect in Japan', *Anthropological Theory*, 1–29.

Genda, Yūji (2005) *A Nagging Sense of Job Insecurity.* Translated by Jean Connell Hoff. Tokyo: International House of Japan.

Goodman, Roger (2005) 'Making Majority Culture', in Jennifer Robertson (ed.) *A Companion to the Anthropology of Japan*, pp. 59–72. Oxford: Blackwell.

Goodman, Roger, ed. (2002) *Family and Social Policy in Japan: Anthropological Approaches.* Cambridge: Cambridge University Press.

Gordon, Andrew (2008) *A Modern History of Japan: From Tokugawa Times to the Present.* New York and Oxford: Oxford University Press.

Gotoh, Megumi (1989) 'Alcohol Dependence of Women in Japan', *Addiction,* 89(8): 953–54.

Gusfield, John (1987) 'Passage to Play: Rituals of Drinking Time in American Society', in Mary Douglas (eds.) *Constructive Drinking: Perspectives on Drink from Anthropology*, pp. 73–90. Cambridge: Cambridge University Press.

Hall, Peter A., and David Soskice, ed. (2001) *Varieties of Capitalism: The Institutional Foundations of Comparative Advantage.* Oxford: Oxford University Press.

Hamada, Tomoko (2005) 'The Anthropology of Japanese Corporate Management', in Jennifer Robertson (ed.) *A Companion to the Anthropology of Japan*, pp. 125–52. Oxford: Blackwell.

Harvey, David (1989) 'From Managerialism to Entrepreneurialism: The Transformation of Urban Governance in Late Capitalism', *Geografiska Annaler,* 71B: 3–17.

Hendry, Joy (1981) *Marriage in Changing Japan: Community and Society.* London: Croom Helm.

Hendry, Joy (1997) 'Drinking and Gender in Japan', in Maryon McDonald (ed.) *Gender, Drink and Drugs*, pp. 175–90. Oxford and New York: Berg.

Higuchi, Susumu, Sachio Matsushita, Hitoshi Maesato and Yoneatsu Osaki (2007) 'Japan: Alcohol Today', *Addiction,* 102(December): 1849–62.

Hinkson, Melinda (2017) 'Precarious Placemaking', *Annual Review of Anthropology,* 46: 49–64.

Ho, Swee-Lin (2008) 'Private Love and Public Space: Love Hotels and the Transformation of Intimacy in Contemporary Japan', *Asian Studies Review,* 32(March): 31–56.

Ho, Swee-Lin (2012a) "Playing Like Men': The Extramarital Experiences of Women in Contemporary Japan', *Ethnos,* 77(3): 321–43.

Ho, Swee-Lin (2012b) 'Tokyo at 10: Establishing Difference through the Friendship Networks of Women Executives in Japan', *Journal of the Royal Anthropological Institute* 18(2): 83–102.

Ho, Swee-Lin (2015) "License to Drink': White-Collar Female Workers and Japan's Urban Night Space', *Ethnography,* 16(1): 25–50.

Ho, Swee-Lin (2018) *Friendship and Work Culture of Women Managers in Japan: Tokyo After Ten.* New York and London: Routledge.

Hochschild, Arlie Russell (1983) *The Managed Heart: Commercialization of Human Feeling.* Berkeley, Los Angeles and London: University of California Press.

Honda, Junko (1984) *Danjo Koyō Kintō Towa Nanika* [What Equal Employment Opportunity Law Is All About]. Tokyo: Daiyamondasha.

Hsiao, Philip (2015) 'Power Harassment: The Tort of Workplace Bullying in Japan', *UCLA Pacific Basin Law Journal,* 32(2): 181–201.

Inoue, Shoichi (1999) *Ai no Kūkan* [Space for Love]. Tokyo: Kadokawasensho.

Ito, Masami (2007) 'Yanagisawa Calls Women "Birth-Giving Machines"'. *The Japan Times*, 28 January. Accessible online at: www.japantimes.co.jp/news/2007/01/28/national/yanagisawa-calls-women-child-bearing-machines/#.WWocPjOB2Ho [accessed 30 September 2019].

Ito, Masami (2014) 'Dealing with Addiction: Japan's Drinking Problem'. *The Japan Times*, 30 August. Accessible online at: www.japantimes.co.jp/life/2014/08/30/lifestyle/dealing-addiction-japans-drinking-problem/#.XScHopMzaF0 [accessed 30 September 2019].

Iwao, Sumiko (1993) *The Japanese Woman: Traditional Image and Changing Reality.* New York: The Free Press.

JapanGov (2014) *We Are Tomodachi* [We Are Friends], (Issue 4, Summer 2014). Tokyo: The Government of Japan.

JapanGov (2017) *We Are Tomodachi* [We Are Friends], (Issue 22, Spring 2017). Tokyo: The Government of Japan.

Ji, Ji (2019) 'LDP Group Mulls Mandatory Measures and Law Revisions to Promote Paternity Leave'. *The Japan Times*, 5 June. Accessible online at: www.japantimes.co.jp/news/2019/06/05/national/ldp-group-mulls-mandatory-measures-law-revisions-promote-paternity-leave/#.XShD8pMzaF0 [accessed 30 September 2019].

JILPT (2017) *Japanese Working Life Profile 2016/2017 – Labor Statistics.* Tokyo: The Japan Institute for Labour Policy and Training, Ministry of Health, Labour and Welfare, Japan.

Kalleberg, Arne L. (2009) 'Precarious Work, Insecure Workers: Employment Relations in Transition', *American Sociological Review,* 74: 1–22.

Kalleberg, Arne L., and Steven P. Vallas (2018) 'Probing Precarious Work: Theory, Research, and Politics', in Arne L. Kalleberg and Steven P. Vallas (eds.) *Precarious Work: Causes, Characteristics, and Consequences (Research in the Sociology of Work)*, pp. 1–30. Bingley, England: Emerald.

Kambayashi, Ryo (2010) 'Dismissal Regulation in Japan', *Global COE Hi-Stat Discussion Paper Series (Hitotsubashi University),* 119: 1–22.

Kawai, Hayao (1976) *Bosei Shakai Nihon no Byōri* [The Pathology of Japan as a Maternal Society]. Tokyo: Chūōkōron Shinsha.

Kawasaki, Takaya (2016) 'Dentsu Head Admits Illegal Labor Practices in Overwork Death'. *NHK World*, 22 September. Accessible online at: www3.nhk.or.jp/nhkworld/en/news/editors/3/dentsuheadadmitsillegallaborpracticesinoverworkdeath/index.html [accessed 30 September 2019].

Keizer, Arjan (2010) *Changes in Japanese Employment Practices: Beyond the Japanese Model.* London and New York: Routledge.

Kim, Hyun Mee (2004) 'Feminization of the 2002 World Cup and Women's Fandom', *Inter-Asia Cultural Studies,* 5(1): 42–51.

Kingston, Jeff (2004) *Japan's Quiet Transformation: Social Change and Civil Society in the Twenty-First Century.* London and New York: RoutledgeCurzon.

Klikauer, Thomas (2015) 'What Is Managerialism?', *Critical Sociology,* 41(7–8): 1103–19.

Kondo, Dorinne K. (1990) *Crafting Selves: Power, Gender, and Discourses of Identity in a Japanese Workplace.* Chicago and London: University of Chicago Press.

Kretsos, Lefteris (2011) 'Union Responses to the Rise of Precarious Youth Employment in Greece', *Industrial Relations Journal,* 42(5): 453–72.

Kumazawa, Noboru (2002) *Make Inu ga Kaetta* [The Loser Dogs Have Returned]. Tokyo: Bungeisha.

Kyodo (2019) 'Japan's Cabinet Adopts Bills to Ban Harassment and Promote Women's Advancement', (8 March 2019). *Kyodo News*, 30 June 2019. Accessible online at: www.japantimes.co.jp/news/2019/03/08/national/japans-cabinet-adopts-bills-ban-harassment-promote-womens-advancement/#.XMbBhZMzaF1 [accessed 30 September 2019].

Kyodo (2019) 'Japan Beefs Up Measures against Workplace Harassment', *Kyodo News,* 29 May 2019. Accessible online at: english.kyodonews.net/news/2019/05/63396d2a82a0-japan-beefs-up-measures-against-workplace-harassment.html [accessed 30 September 2019].

Lam, Alice (1993) 'Equal Employment Opportunities for Japanese Women: Changing Company Practice', in Jane Hunter (ed.) *Japanese Working Women*, pp. 197–223. London and New York: Routledge.

Lan, Pei-Chia (2002) 'Among Women: Migrant Domestics and Their Taiwanese Employers', in Barbara Ehrenreich and Arlie Russell Hochschild (eds.) *Global Woman: Nannies, Maids, and Sex Workers in the New Economy*, pp. 169–89. London: Granta.

Le Goff, Jean-Pierre (1996) *Le Mythe de l'entreprise. Critique de l'idéologie managériale* [The Myth of the Company: Criticism of the Managerial Ideology]. Paris: La Découverte.

Lebra, Takie Sugiyama (1984) *Japanese Women: Constraint and Fulfillment.* Honolulu: University of Hawai'i Press.

Linhart, Sepp (1998) '*Sakariba*: Zone of 'Evaporation' Between Work and Home?', in Joy Hendry and Jonathan Webber (eds.) *Interpreting Japanese Society: Anthropological Approaches*, pp. 231–42. London: Routledge.

LSA (1947, 7 April) *Exclusion from Application of Provisions on Working Hours, etc.* Act No. 49 vols. Vol. Article 41. *Labor Standards Act*. Japan.

Mabuchi, Ryogo (2007) 'How Labor Unions Are Perceived by Members and Union Disassociation in Japan', *Japan Labor Review,* 4(1): 91–111.

Mackie, Vera (2003) *Feminism in Modern Japan*. Cambridge: Cambridge University Press.

Marx, W. David (2010) 'Manabu Numata: Chronicling Tokyo's Host Clubs', *CNN*, 25 March. Accessible online at: www.cnngo.com/tokyo/play/manabu-numata-chronicling-tokyos-host-clubs-784426 [accessed 30 September 2019].

Matos, Patricia (2019) 'Locating Precarization: The State, Livelihoods and the Politics of Precarity in Contemporary Portugal', *Dialectical Anthropology,* 43: 15–30.

Matsui, Kathy, Hiromi Suzuki, and Kazunori Tatebe (2019) *Womenomics 5.0: Progress, Areas for Improvement, Potential 15% GDP Boost*. New York: Goldman Sachs Group.

Matsui, Kathy, Hiromi Suzuki, Christopher Eoyang, Tsumugi Akiba, and Kazunori Tatebe (2010) *Womenomics 3.0: The Time Is Now.* New York: Goldman Sachs Group.

Matsunaga, Louella (2000) *The Changing Face of Japanese Retail*. London and New York: Routledge.

McCormack, Donna, and Suvi Salmenniemi (2017) 'The Biopolitics of Precarity and the Self', *European Journal of Cultural Studies,* 19(1): 3–15.

McCurry, Justin (2018) 'Shinzo Abe Reshuffle Leaves Just One Woman in Japanese Cabinet'. *The Guardian*, 3 October. Accessible online at: www.theguardian.com/world/2018/oct/03/shinzo-abe-reshuffle-leaves-just-one-woman-in-japanese-cabinet-satsuki-katayama [accessed 30 September 2019].

MHLW (2012a) *Heisei 24 Nendo Kobetsu Rōdōfunsō Kaiketsu Seido Shikō Jōkyō* [2012 Report on the Resolution System for Individual Labour Disputes]. Tokyo: Ministry of Health, Labour and Welfare, Japan.

MHLW (2012b) *Shokuba no Pawā Harasumento ni Kansuru Jittai Chōsa* [A Survey of the Actual Conditions of Power Harassment in the Workplace]. Tokyo: Ministry of Health, Labour and Welfare, Japan.

MHLW (2013) *Shokuba no Pawā Harasumento Taisaku Hanobukku* [Handbook for Policies on Power Harassment in the Workplace]. Tokyo: Ministry of Health, Labour and Welfare, Japan.

Millar, Kathleen (2014) 'The Precarious Present: Wageless Labor and Disrupted Life in Rio de Janeiro, Brazil', *Cultural Anthropology,* 29(1): 32–53.

Misago, Chizuru (2004) *Onibabaka suru Onnatachi* [The Trend of Women Becoming Demonic Hags]. Tokyo: Kōbunsha.

Miura, Atsushi (2005) *Karyū Shakai* [Downward Drifting Society]. Tokyo: Kōbunsha.

Miyoshi, Masao, and Harry D. Harootunian, eds. (1989) *Postmodernism in Japan*. Durham and London: Duke University Press.

Mizuno, Asao (1984) *Keizai Sofu toka Jidai no Josei no Rōdō: Nichi Bei Ō no Keiken* [The Service Economy and Women's Employment: The Japanese, American and European Experiences]. Tokyo: Yūkikaku Sensho.

Mizushima, Ikuko (2013) 'Workplace Harassment, Mental Health, and the Law', *Japan Labor Review,* 10(3): 40–55.

Moeran, Brian (1998) 'One Over the Seven: Sake Drinking in a Japanese Pottery Community', in Joy Hendry and Jonathan Webber (eds.) *Interpreting Japanese Society: Anthropological Approaches*, pp. 243–58. London: Routledge.

MOFA (2015) *Creating 'A Society Where Women Can Shine'*. Tokyo: Ministry of Foreign Affairs, Japan.

MOL (1981) *Joshi Rōdōsha no Oyō Anri ni Kansuru Chōsa* [A Survey on the Employment and Management of Female Workers]. Tokyo: Rōdōshō Fujin Kyoku (Women's Bureau), Ministry of Labour, Japan.

Molony, Barbara (1995) 'Japan's 1986 Equal Employment Opportunity Law and the Changing Discourse on Gender', *Signs,* 20(2): 286–302.

Moriya, Takashi (2005) *Nihon Kigyō e no Seika-Shugi Dōnyū: Kigyōnai Kyōdōtai no Henyō* [Introduction of *Seika-Shugi* to Japanese Corporations: Changing Corporate Communities]. Tokyo: Moriyama Shoten.

Mouer, Ross, and Yoshio Sugimoto (1986) *Images of Japanese Society: A Study in the Structure of Social Reality.* London, New York, Sydney and Henley: KPI.

Muehlebach, Andrea (2012) 'On Precariousness and the Ethical Imagination: The Year 2012 in Sociocultural Anthropology', *American Anthropologist,* 115(2): 297–311.

Nader, Laura (1972) 'Up the Anthropologist: Perspectives Gained from Studying Up', in Dell Hymes (ed.) *Reinventing Anthropology*, pp. 284–311. New York: Pantheon Books.

Nader, Laura (1997) 'Controlling Processes: Tracing the Dynamic Components of Power', *Current Anthropology,* 38(5): 711–38.

Naito, Shino (2013) 'Workplace Bullying in Japan', *JILPT Report,* 12: 113–33.

Nakamura, Keisuke (2007) 'Decline or Revival?: Japanese Labor Unions', *Japan Labor Review,* 4(1): 7–22.

Nakamura, Tadashi (2003) 'Re-Gendering Batterers: Domestic Violence and Men's Movements', in James E. Roberson and Nobue Suzuki (eds.) *Men and Masculinities in Contemporary Japan: Dislocating the Salaryman Doxa*, pp. 162–79. London and New York: RoutledgeCurzon.

Nakane, Chie (1967) *Tateshakai no Ningen Kankei: Tan Ichi Shakai no Riron* [Human Relations in a Vertical Society]. Tokyo: Kodansha.

Nakane, Chie (1970) *Japanese Society.* Berkeley, Los Angeles and London: University of California Press.

Nemoto, Kumiko (2013) 'Long Working Hours and the Corporate Gender Divide in Japan', *Gender, Work and Organization*, 20(5): 512–27

Nikkei (2018) '*Pawahara bōshi kigyō no gimu ni kōrōshō ga hōseibi e* [Preparations by The Ministry of Health, Labour and Welfare to Legalize Power Harassment Prevention as the Responsibility of Companies]'. *Nihon Keizai Shimbun*, 19 November. Accessible online at: www.nikkei.com/article/DGXMZO37940190Z11C18A1EE8000/ [accessed 30 September 2019].

Nomura, Masami (2000) 'Seika-Shugi no Otoshiana: Shinjinjiseido wo Kangaeru [Pitfalls of Seika-Shugi: Rethinking the New Personnel System]', *Rōseijihō*, 3462: 11–16.

OECD (2017) *Health at a Glance.* Paris: OECD Publishing.

OECD (2018) *OECD Employment Outlook 2018.* Paris: OECD Publishing.

Ogasawara, Yuko (1998) *Office Ladies and Salaried Men: Power, Gender, and Work in Japanese Companies.* Berkeley, Los Angeles and London: University of California Press.

Ogura, Kazuya (2010) 'Managerial Working Hours and Heavy Workloads', *Japan Labor Review,* 7(4): 45–71.

Olcott, George (2010) *Conflict and Change: Foreign Ownership and the Japanese Firm.* Cambridge and New York: Cambridge University Press.

Ortner, Sherry B. (1998) 'Generation X: Anthropology in a Media-Saturated World', *Cultural Anthropology,* 13(3): 414–40.

Ortner, Sherry B. (1999) *Life and Death on Mt Everest: Sherpas and Himalayan Mountaineering.* Princeton and Oxford: Princeton University Press.

Osawa, Machiko (2005) 'Japan's Changing Economy and Women Workers', *The Japanese Economy,* 32(4): 96–108.

Ouchi, Shinya (2008) ''Nabakari Kanrishoku' Mondai no Taikakeru Mono [Questions Raised by the Issue of Nominal Management]', *The Japanese Journal of Labour Studies,* 47(12): 4–17.

Ouchi, Shinya (2010) 'Legal Issues Concerning Nominal Supervisors and Managers', *Japan Labor Review,* 7(4): 72–83.

Ōwaki, Masako (1987) *Kintōhō Jidai wo Ikiru* [Living in the Era of the Equal Employment Opportunity Law]. Tokyo: Yuikaku.

Ozaki, Masaya (2005) *Jitsuroku Oniyome Nikki: Aisarete Okanemochi ni naru* [True Accounts of the Demonic Daughter-in-Law: Becoming Rich When You Are Being Loved]. Tokyo: Amoeba Books.

Ozaki, Masaya (2006a) *Jitsuroku Oniyome Nikki 1* [True Accounts of the Demonic Daughter-in-Law 1]. Tokyo: Shuesha.

Ozaki, Masaya (2006b) *Jitsuroku Oniyome Nikki 2* [True Accounts of the Demonic Daughter-in-Law 2]. Tokyo: Shuesha.

Parreñas, Rhacel Salazar (2002) 'The Care Crisis in the Philippines: Children and the Transnational Families in the New Global Economy', in Barbara Ehrenreich and Arlie Russell Hochschild (eds.) *Global Woman: Nannies, Maids, and Sex Workers in the New Economy,* pp. 39–54. London: Granta.

Rebick, Marcus (2005) *The Japanese Employment System: Adapting to a New Economic Environment.* Oxford: Oxford University Press.

Roberson, James E., and Nobue Suzuki, eds. (2003) *Men and Masculinities in Contemporary Japan: Dislocating the Salaryman Doxa.* London and New York: RoutledgeCurzon.

Roberts, Glenda S. (1994) *Staying on the Line: Blue Collar Women in Contemporary Japan.* Honolulu: University of Hawai'i Press.

Roberts, Glenda S. (2005) 'Shifting Contours of Class and Status', in Jennifer Robertson (ed.) *A Companion to the Anthropology of Japan,* pp. 104–24. Oxford: Blackwell.

Roberts, Glenda S. (2011) 'Salary Women and Family Well-Being in Urban Japan', *Marriage & Family Review,* 47: 571–89.

Roberts, Glenda S. (2014) ''Power Harassment' and the Workplace Environment in Japan: The Evolution of the Concept Amidst Uncertain Times', *Journal of Asia-Pacific Studies,* 22(March): 21–35.

Sakai, Junko (2001) *Make Inu no Tōboe* [Howls of the Loser Dog]. Tokyo: Kodansha.

Sakai, Naoki (1989) 'Modernity and Its Critique: The Problem of Universalism and Particularism', in Masao Miyoshi and Harry D. Harootunian (eds.) *Postmodernism in Japan,* pp. 93–122. Durham and London: Duke University Press.

Sarada, Tamako (1998) *Parasaito Shinguru* [Parasite Singles]. Tokyo: WAVE.

Seigle, Cecilia Segawa (1991) *Yoshiwara: The Glittering World of the Japanese Courtesan.* Honolulu: University of Hawai'i Press.

Sennett, Richard (2000) 'Street and Office: Two Sources of Identity', in Will Hutton and Anthony Giddens (eds.) *Global Capitalism,* pp. 175–90. New York: The New Press.

Shimizu, Tatsuo (2005) *Make Inu* [The Loser Dog]. Tokyo: Kodansha.

Shirai, Toshiaki (2005) *Meisōsuru Wakamono no Aidentiti* [The Lost Identities of Youths]. Tokyo: Yumani Shobō.

Shirakawa, Toko (2019) 'Why Paternity Leave Should be Mandatory'. *The Japan Times*, 14 June. Accessible online at: www.japantimes.co.jp/opinion/2019/06/14/commentary/japan-commentary/paternity-leave-mandatory/#.XShFPpMzaF0 [accessed 30 September 2019].

SHJ (2018) *Statistical Handbook of Japan 2018*. Tokyo: Ministry of Internal Affairs and Communications, Japan.

Shoji, Kaori (2019) 'Chemical Firm Hit for Punishing Worker Who Took Paternity Leave with Transfer Halfway Across Japan'. *The Japan Times*, 7 June. Accessible online at: www.japantimes.co.jp/news/2019/06/07/national/media-national/chemical-manufacturer-kaneka-fire-paternity-harassment-allegations/#.XShF6ZMzaF0 [accessed 30 September 2019].

Shoji, Kaori (2019) 'Be Aware of Japanese Workplace No-Nos'. *The Japan Times*, 30 September. Accessible online at: www.japantimes.co.jp/news/2019/06/07/national/media-national/chemical-manufacturer-kaneka-fire-paternity-harassment-allegations/#.XShF6ZMzaF0 [accessed 30 September 2019].

Skachkova, Penka (2007) 'Academic Careers of Immigrant Women Professors in the US', *Higher Education*, 53: 697–738.

Slater, David H. (2010) 'The "New Working Class" of Urban Japan: Socialization and Contradiction from Middle School to the Labor Market', in Hiroshi Ishida and David H. Slater (eds.) *Social Class in Contemporary Japan: Structures, Sorting and Srategies*, pp. 137–69. London and New York: Routledge.

Slater, David H., and Patrick W. Galbraith (2011) Re-Narrating Social Class and Masculinity in Neoliberal Japan. *Electronic Journal of Contemporary Japanese Studies*, www.japanesestudies.org.uk/articles/2011/SlaterGalbraith.html.

Spivak, Gayatri Chakravorty (1988) 'Can the Subaltern Speak?', in Cary Nelson and Lawrence Grossberg (eds.) *Marxism and the Interpretation of Culture*, pp. 271–313. Urbana: University of Illinois Press.

Steinhoff, Patricia G., and Kazuko Tanaka (1993) 'Women Managers in Japan', *International Studies of Management & Organization*, 23(2): 25–48.

Sugeno, Kazuo, and Keiichi Yamakoshi (2014a) 'Dismissals in Japan (Part One): How Strict Is Japanese Law on Employers?', *Japan Labor Review*, 11(2) 83–92.

Sugeno, Kazuo, and Keiichi Yamakoshi (2014b) 'Dismissals in Japan (Part Two): How Strict Is Japanese Law on Employers?', *Japan Labor Review*, 11(4): 118–37.

Suzuki, Takaaki (2015) 'After Neoliberalism? The Curious Non-Death of Neoliberalism in Japan', *Asian Journal of Social Science*, 43(1/2): 151–77.

Suzuki, Yukari (2002) *Rabu Hoteru no Chikara* [The Power of Love Hotels]. Tokyo: Kosaido.

Takada, Masatoshi (1983) *Sakariba no Shakaigaku* [A Social Study of Sakariba]. Tokyo: PHP.

Takahashi, Kenji (2005) 'Kanrishoku no Koyo Kankei to Ho (Employment Relations of Managerial Employees and Law)', *The Japanese Journal of Labour Studies*, 47(12): 18–28.

Takano, Takehito, Keiko Nakamura and Masafumi Watanabe (1996) 'Increased Female Drinking In Accordance With Post-Industrial Urbanization in Japan', *Alcohol & Alcoholism*, 31(1): 41–49.

Tanaka, Michiko (1984) *Danjo Koyō Byōdōhō wo Meguru Jōsei* [Conditions Surrounding the Male-Female Employment Equality Law]. Tokyo: Gakushu no Yūsha.

Tatsumichi, Shingo, and Motoharu Morishima (2004) 'Haken Rōdōsha no Jinzai Manejimento no Kadai [Issues in HR Management of Dispatch Workers]', *Nihon Rōdō Kenkyū Zasshi*, 526: 4–15.

Thorkelson, Eli (2016) 'Precarity Outside: The Political Unconscious of French Academic Labor', *American Ethnologist,* 43(3): 475–87.

Tiberghien, Yves (2014) 'Thirty Years of Neo-Liberal Reforms in Japan', in: Sébastien Lechevalier (ed.) *The Great Transformation of Japanese Capitalism*, pp. 26–55. London and New York: Routledge.

Tomīzu, Ken (2008) *Tomīzu Ken no Yomesan Nikki: Boku no 'Oniyome' Daiarii* [Tomīzu Ken's Diary About His Wife: My *Oniyome* Diary]. Tokyo: Uni Books.

UNICEF (2019) *Are the World's Richest Countries Family Friendly?* Florence: United Nations Children's Fund (UNICEF).

Uno, Kathleen (1993) 'Death of 'Good Wife, Wise Mother'?', in Andrew Gordon (ed.) *Postwar Japan as History*, pp. 293–322. Berkeley, Los Angeles and London: University of California Press.

Valentine, James (1990) 'On the Borderlines: The Significance of Marginality in Japanese Society', in Brian Moeran and James Valentine Eyal Ben-Ari (eds.) *Unwrapping Japan: Society and Culture in Anthropological Perspective*, pp. 36–57. Honolulu: University of Hawai'i Press.

Vogel, Ezra F. (1971[1963]) *Japan's New Middle Class: The Salary Men and His Family in a Tokyo Suburb.* Berkeley: University of California Press.

Vosko, Leah Faith (2000) *Temporary Work: The Gendered Rise of a Precarious Employment Relationship.* Toronto: University of Toronto Press.

Vosko, Leah Faith (2011) *Managing the Margins: Gender, Citizenship, and the International Regulation of Precarious Employment.* Oxford: Oxford University Press.

Wada, Hideki (2004) *Parasaito Daburu nara Umakuiku* [How to be Good at Becoming A Parasite Double]. Tokyo: PHP Kenkyūjo.

Waswo, Ann (1996) *Modern Japanese Society 1868–1994.* Oxford and New York: Oxford University Press.

Weber, Max (1958) *The Rise of Protestant Ethics and the Spirit of Capitalism.* New York: Charles Scribner's Sons.

White, Merry (2002) *Perfectly Japanese: Making Families in an Era of Upheaval.* Berkeley: University of California Press.

Yamada, Masahiro (1999) *Parasaito Shinguru no Jidai* [The Age of the Parasite Single]. Tokyo: Chikuma Shinsho.

Yamaguchi, Tomomi (2006) ''Loser Dogs' and 'Demon Hags': Single Women in Japan and the Declining Birth Rate', *Social Science Japan Journal,* 9(1): 109–14.

Yamazaki, Makiko (2006) *Tōkyō Make Inu Kyōshikyoku* [The Mad Songs of Tokyo's Loser Dogs]. Tokyo: JTB Puburishingu.

Yashiro, Atsushi (2002) 'Naze 'Nabakari Kanrishoku' ga Umarerunoka [On the Mechanism of Managers 'Disguised' in Japanese Companies]', *The Japanese Journal of Labour Studies,* 51(4): 38–41.

Yoda, Tomiko (2006) 'The Rise and Fall of Maternal Society: Gender, Labor, and Capital in Contemporary Japan', in Tomiko Yoda and Harry Harootunian (eds.) *Japan After Japan: Social and Cultural Life from the Recessionary 1990s to the Present*, pp. 239–74. Durham and London: Duke University Press.

Yoshikawa, Eiichiro (2017) 'Harassment Law in Japan and Trends in Recent Cases', *Doshisha Daigaku Shogakkai,* 66(3–4): 530–48.

Yuasa, Masae (2005) 'Japanese Women in Management: Getting Closer to 'Realities' in Japan', *Asia Pacific Business Review,* 11(2): 195–211.

Žižek, Slavoj (2012) 'The Revolt of the Salaried Bourgeoisie', *London Review of Books,* 34(2): 9–10.

Index

Note: *italic* page numbers refer to figures and page numbers followed by "n" denote endnotes.

For Product Safety Concerns and Information please contact our EU
representative GPSR@taylorandfrancis.com
Taylor & Francis Verlag GmbH, Kaufingerstraße 24, 80331 München, Germany

www.ingramcontent.com/pod-product-compliance
Lightning Source LLC
LaVergne TN
LVHW021109300926
849160LV00009B/658

9781032174617